Globalization and the Poor Periphery before 1950

The Ohlin Lectures

1. Jagdish Bhagwati, *Protectionism* (1988)

2. Richard N. Cooper, *Economic Stabilization and Debt in Developing Countries* (1992)

3. Assar Lindbeck, *Unemployment and Macroeconomics* (1993)

4. Anne O. Krueger, *Political Economy of Policy Reform in Developing Countries* (1993)

5. Ronald Findlay, *Factor Proportions, Trade, and Growth* (1995)

6. Paul Krugman, *Development, Geography, and Economic Theory* (1995)

7. Deepak K. Lal, *Unintended Consequences: The Impact of Factor Endowments, Culture, and Politics on Long-Run Economic Performance* (1998)

8. Ronald W. Jones, *Globalization and the Theory of Input Trade* (2000)

9. W. Max Corden, *Too Sensational: On the Choice of Exchange Rate Regimes* (2002)

10. Jeffrey G. Williamson, *Globalization and the Poor Periphery before 1950* (2006)

**Globalization and
the Poor Periphery
before 1950**

Jeffrey G. Williamson

The MIT Press
Cambridge, Massachusetts
London, England

© 2006 Massachusetts Institute of Technology

MIT Press books may be purchased at special quantity discounts for business or sales promotional use. For information, please e-mail <special_sales@mitpress.mit.edu> or write to Special Sales Department, The MIT Press, 55 Hayward Street, Cambridge, MA 02142.

This book was set in Palatino by SNP Best-set Typesetter Ltd., Hong Kong, and printed and bound in the United States of America.

Library of Congress Cataloging-in-Publication Data

Williamson, Jeffrey G., 1935–
Globalization and the poor periphery before 1950 / Jeffrey G. Williamson.
    p. cm.—(Ohlin ectures ; 10)
Includes bibliographical references and index.
ISBN 0-262-23250-2 (hc : alk. paper)
1. Developing countries—Economic conditions—20th century. 2. Industrialization—History—20th century. 3. Globalization—History—20th century. 4. Economic history—20th century. I. Title. II. Series.
HC59.7.W535   2006   337′.09172′409041—dc22   2005054002

10 9 8 7 6 5 4 3 2 1

In memory and recognition of three giants
upon whose shoulders these lectures stand:
Moses Abramovitz
Bertil Ohlin
William Arthur Lewis

Contents

Acknowledgments

This book is a revision of the Ohlin Lectures given at the Stockholm School of Economics, October 11–12, 2004. The lectures draw heavily on my past and current work on Third World globalization and history undertaken with many collaborators, some of whom have been my students, but all of whom are close friends. I am immensely grateful to them all: Luis Bértola, Chris Blattman, Michael Clemens, David Clingingsmith, John Coatsworth, Bill Collins, Yael Hadass, Tim Hatton, Jason Hwang, Peter Lindert, Saif Shah Mohammed, Kevin O'Rourke, Şevket Pamuk, and Alan Taylor.

As will become apparent to any economist trained in international economics, these lectures use the tools first constructed by Bertil Ohlin almost a century ago (himself standing on the shoulders of Eli Heckscher). Indeed, much of the economic history that these lectures explore are the very same decades that motivated what has come to be called Heckscher-Ohlin and Stolper-Samuelson economics. Furthermore, as will become apparent to anyone who has read his works, these lectures have also been motivated by and draw heavily on the pioneering and lasting contributions by William Arthur Lewis to our understanding of modern economic growth. Lewis made his contributions at that critical point where theory, history, and policy intersect, most famously manifested by the publication of his labor surplus paper in 1954 almost a half-century ago, and capped by his Janeway Lectures in 1977. Last, these lectures bear the mark of my teacher, Moses Abramovitz, a great scholar who, when I was a graduate student at Stanford more than four decades ago, showed me how his powerful mix of theory and history can be used to understand the connections between growth and globalization. These Ohlin Lectures are offered in the memory of these three giants who have had such a profound impact on my thinking—Bertil Ohlin, William Arthur Lewis, and Moses Abramovitz.

I also want to thank the National Science Foundation for support of my globalization and history research over the years, especially most recently under NSF grant SES-0001362.

Finally, I want to thank my Swedish hosts, the Ohlin family and the faculty at the Stockholm School of Economics. In particular, my thanks go to Lars Bergman, Rektor at the Stockholm School, and Mats Lundahl, a good friend who managed the event, held my hand during the process, and attended to all the local arrangements with skill, calm, and humor.

Cambridge, Massachusetts
Summer 2005

Globalization and the Poor Periphery before 1950

1

Laws of Motion: Secular Boom and Bust in the Premodern Periphery

These Ohlin Lectures define the core as northwest Europe and their overseas settlements, regions where the industrial revolution started and then took off across the nineteenth century. The periphery includes the rest—industrially lagging Europe to the east and south of the core, the Middle East, Africa, Asia, and Latin America. The premodern era is defined as the first global century, about 1820 to 1913, plus the antiglobal, autarkic interwar, 1914–1940.

The economic impact of the core on the periphery had its source in two forces that arose during the first global century. The first was a worldwide transport revolution that served to integrate world commodity markets. It caused a boom in trade between core and periphery, created commodity price convergence for tradable goods between all world markets, and contributed to a rise in every country's external terms of trade, including the periphery, indeed, especially in the periphery. The second force came from the derived demand for primary product intermediates, such as cotton and metals, which soared as manufacturing production led the way in the core. Rapid productivity growth lowered the cost and price of manufactures, and by so doing generated a soaring derived demand for raw materials in the core. This event was reinforced by accelerating income per capita growth and a high elasticity of demand for luxury consumption goods, such as meat, tea, and coffee. Since industrialization was driven by unbalanced productivity advances favoring manufacturing relative to agriculture and other natural resource–based activities, the relative price of manufactures fell everywhere, especially in the periphery where they were imported.

The world transport revolution made it possible for the distant periphery to supply this booming demand for primary products in the core. Both forces produced positive, powerful, and sustained terms-of-trade shocks in the periphery, raising the relative price of primary products, and through an epoch that stretched over as much as seventy years. Factor supply responses in the periphery facilitated these external demand shocks, carried by south–south migration from labor-abundant to labor-scarce regions in the periphery and by financial capital flows from the core to those same regions. When these two forces abated, and when that abatement was joined by resource-saving innovations in the core (induced, in large part, by those high and rising primary product prices), the secular boom faded, eventually turning into a secular bust. Finally, whether during boom or bust, technological advance and human capital accumulation were so modest in the periphery that the living standard gap between it and the core surged to levels that were vastly wider at the end of the cycle than when it started almost a century and a half before. Whether the modest rates of technological advance and human capital accumulation in the periphery were caused at least partly by globalization-induced deindustrialization forces there has, of course, been a central issue in growth and development debate since it all started.

Between 1820 and 1940, the periphery obeyed laws of motion that economists delight in exploring. The long-run secular boom and bust was generated in response to two of the most profound technological shocks the world had yet seen—in industry and transportation, shocks exogenous to the periphery, if not the core.

These lectures document these laws of motion in the periphery, assess their distribution and growth consequences, and then ask how trade policy responded to them.

I

Impact on Prices, Trade, and Distribution

Core Growth and World Transport Revolutions

World Transport Revolutions in the First Global Century

The Great Transition

Until well into the nineteenth century, the cost of overseas trade was simply too great to allow much long-distance trade in bulky primary products. Thus, most foodstuffs and most industrial intermediates were nontradables—their prices determined in local markets—and most long-distance trade between core and periphery involved only precious metals and the consumption goods of the rich. These tradables were typically noncompeting; that is, they were not produced in local markets and thus their import did not directly crowd out any local industry (O'Rourke and Williamson 2002a, 2005). In spite of all the attention that the Age of Discovery and the Age of Commerce get from historians, the descriptive phrase "global economy" only applied to a tiny share of world economic activity before the nineteenth century. Nor is there much evidence suggesting that world market integration took place between 1492 and 1820. World prices did not converge between Asian, American, and European markets, since trading monopolies did what monopolies do so well: they choked off trade by internalizing falling transport costs, and by keeping the price markup between producer and consumer high or even rising (O'Rourke and Williamson 2002b).

A great transition took place between about 1820 and 1860 that changed global factor and commodity markets completely. As the trading monopolies were replaced by competitive firms and competitive markets, the world economy became qualitatively more globally integrated, and by the end of the period most nontradable primary products had become tradables. This great transition involved a transport revolution over both water and land, and the periphery played a very important part in it, indeed, perhaps the most important part.

Investment in river and harbor improvements increased briskly in the European core following the French Wars, but it had its start in the mid-eighteenth century. British navigable waterways quadrupled between 1750 and 1820 and canals offered a transport option 50–75 percent cheaper than roads. On the European continent, French canal construction boomed, while the Congress of Vienna recognized freedom of navigation on the Rhine. In the United States, construction of the Erie Canal between 1817 and 1825 reduced the cost of transport between Buffalo and New York by 85 percent, and cut the transit time from 21 to 8 days. The rates between Baltimore and Cincinnati fell by 58 percent from 1821 to 1860 and by 92 percent between Louisville and New Orleans from 1816 and 1860. While it took fifty-two days to ship a load of freight from Cincinnati to New York by wagon and riverboat in 1817, it took only six days in 1852. The U.S. internal transport sector recorded productivity growth rates something like 4.7 percent per annum in the four decades or so before the Civil War (Williamson and

Lindert 1980). As a result, regional price differentials under-went a spectacular fall from as high as 100 percent to as low as 10 percent (Slaughter 1995: 13). In the four or five decades prior to 1860, transportation improvements began to destroy regional barriers to internal trade and integrated national goods markets began to emerge within the United States, within Britain, within the German *Zollverein*, and within other countries on the continent.

Steamships made the most important contribution to nineteenth-century shipping technology. The *Claremont* made its debut on the Hudson in 1807; a steamer had made the journey up the Mississippi as far as Louisville by 1815; and steamers had traveled up the Seine to Paris by 1816. In the first half of the century, steamships were mainly used on important rivers, the Great Lakes, and inland seas such as the Baltic and the Mediterranean. A regular transatlantic steam service was inaugurated in 1838, but until 1860 steam-ers mainly carried high-value goods similar to those carried by airplanes today, including passengers, specie, mail, and gourmet food.

The other major nineteenth-century transportation development was, of course, the railroad. The Liverpool-Manchester line opened in 1830, and early continental emu-lators included Belgium, France, and Germany. Table 2.1 documents the phenomenal growth in railway mileage during the second half of the nineteenth century, particu-larly in the United States, where it played a major role in creating a truly national market. Indeed, the railroad was, in many ways, to the United States what the 1992 Single Market program was to the European Union. But the impor-tant point is what is missing in the table: there are no rail-road mileage statistics to report for 1830, an amount too trivial to report for 1840. But by 1850, there are more than

Table 2.1
Railway Mileage, 1850–1910

Country	1850	1870	1890	1910
Austria-Hungary	954	5,949	16,489	26,834
Australia	—	953	9,524	17,429
Argentina	—	637	5,434	17,381
Canada	66	2,617	13,368	26,462
China	—	—	80	5,092
France	1,714	1,142	22,911	30,643
Germany	3,637	11,729	25,411	36,152
India	—	4,771	16,401	32,099
Italy	265	3,825	8,163	10,573
Japan	—	—	1,139	5,130
Mexico	—	215	6,037	15,350
Russia (in Europe)	310	7,098	18,059	34,990
United Kingdom	6,621	15,537	20,073	23,387
United States	9,021	52,922	116,703	249,902

Source: Hurd (1975: appendix 2, 278).

1,700 railroad miles to report for France, more than 3,600 for
Germany, more than 6,600 for the United Kingdom, and
more than 9,000 for the United States. Note also the tiny railroad mileage entries for Austria-Hungary, Italy, and
Russia—and their complete absence before 1870 for Bulgaria
and Romania, or for Portugal and Spain, or for Greece
(Mitchell 1978: 315–318)—facts that helped to postpone the
involvement of the European periphery in the Atlantic
boom until the second half of the century. But by the 1850s,
every major port in the northwest of Europe was within
relatively inexpensive reach of its small town and rural
hinterland.

To get a sense of the timing and magnitude of the transport revolution in the Atlantic economy, consider figure 2.1.

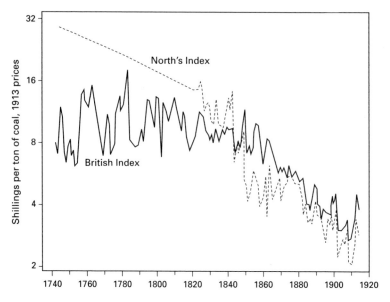

Figure 2.1
Real freight rate indexes 1741–1913
Source: Harley (1988: figure 1), nominal rates divided by a U.K. GDP deflator.

What is labeled North's index (attributed to Douglass North [1958]) accelerates its fall after the 1830s—its most dramatic decline by far being 1840 to 1860, and what is labeled the British index (Harley 1988) exhibits no trend at all up to 1810, after which it underwent the same, big fall. The North index measures freight rates along Atlantic routes connecting American to European ports, and it dropped by almost 55 percent in real terms between the 1830s and 1850s, while other evidence documents a fall in nominal rates of 75 percent between Antwerp and New York (Prados 2004: 10–11). The British index measures major trade routes involving Liverpool and London, and it fell by about 70 percent, again in real terms, in the half century after 1840. These two indices imply a steady decline in Atlantic economy transport costs of about 1.5 percent per annum, for a total of 45 percentage points up to 1913, a big number indeed. One way to get a comparative feel for the magnitude of this decline is to note that tariffs on manufactures entering OECD markets fell from 40 percent in the late 1940s to 7 percent in the late 1970s, a 33 percentage-point decline over this thirty-year resurrection of free trade in the industrial economies. This spectacular postwar reclamation of free trade from interwar autarky is still smaller than the 45 percentage-point fall in trade barriers induced by transport improvements over sea lanes between 1870 and 1913. Furthermore, since the impact of railroads was probably even more important than transport improvements on ocean shipping, that big 45 percentage-point fall is almost certainly an understatement. In addition, it was probably even bigger in the two or three decades before 1870 than afterward.

World Transportation: From Transition to Revolution

What had been a transition in the Atlantic economy until about 1860 became a ubiquitous transport revolution worldwide as these new transport technologies diffused rapidly to the periphery in the half century that followed.

Steamships made the most important contribution to improved shipping technology. As I noted before, steamers mainly carried high-value goods until around 1860. A series of innovations changed all that in subsequent decades: the screw propeller, the compound engine, steel hulls, bigger ships, more efficient crews, increased fuel efficiency, more ships, more predictable schedules, and shorter turnaround time in port—all served to produce a spectacular fall in intercontinental transport costs. Furthermore, the opening of the Suez Canal in 1869 halved the distance from London to Bombay, and the Panama Canal in 1914 cut the distance from New York to Shanghai. Refrigeration was another innovation with major trade implications. In 1876, the first refrigerated ship sailed from Argentina to France carrying frozen beef and by the 1880s Australian meat and New Zealand butter were being exported in large quantities to Europe.

The transport revolution was not limited to the Atlantic economy. The decline in freight rates was just as dramatic on routes involving Black Sea and Egyptian ports, and perhaps even more so (Harlaftis and Kardasis 2000). Even over the fifty years before 1870, freight rates fell by 51 percent along routes connecting Odessa with England (Harley 1988: table 9). And after 1870, the railroads had a big impact in Eurasia and Asia, too. They tied the Ukraine interior wheat lands with Odessa, the Black Sea, and thus with world markets. The same was true of Latin America, and the impact was felt even earlier there. Freight rates between Antwerp and Rio de Janeiro fell by 40 percent from 1820 to 1850, and those between Antwerp and Valparaiso in the Pacific fell by 40 percent from 1850 to 1870 (Prados 2004: 11).

Asia was probably affected most dramatically by the transport revolution. Except for "exotic" products like silk, fine cottons, spices, porcelain, and precious metals, distance seemed almost to have isolated Asian producers and consumers from Europe until well into the nineteenth century.[1] By 1914, transport innovations had erased much of that isolation, and for the first time in recorded history, railroads served to moderate local famines on the Indian subcontinent by connecting regional grain markets (Hurd 1975; MacAlpin

1979). True, the Suez Canal, cost-reducing innovations on seagoing transport, and railroads penetrating the interior did not completely liberate Asia from the tyranny of distance.[2] But it was the change in the economic distance to the European core that mattered to the Asian periphery, even though the costs-to-market remained relatively high, and trade shares in GDP remained relatively low,[3] well into the twentieth century. And those changes were spectacular. An Indonesian freight rate index divided by an export price index fell by 83 percent between 1825 and 1875, and by another 45 percent between 1875 and 1912 (Korthals Altes 1994: 159–60). To take another example, the tramp charter rate for shipping rice from Rangoon (Burma) to Europe fell from 74 to 18 percent of the Rangoon price between 1882 and 1914, and the freight rate on sugar between Java (Dutch East Indies) and Amsterdam fell by 50 or 60 percent. And while the Suez Canal had a profound impact in connecting Europe with Asia, there were equally dramatic changes taking place within Asia. For example, the freight rate on shipping coal from Nagasaki (Japan) to Shanghai (China) fell by 76 percent between 1880 and 1910, and total factor productivity on Japan's tramp freighter routes serving Asia advanced at an amazing 2.5 percent per annum between 1879 and 1909 (Yasuba 1978: tables 1 and 3).

Railroads were an important part of the transport technologies that contributed so much to world market integration in the century before World War I. Furthermore, in many parts of the periphery they were even more important than they were in the core. Economic historians reading these lectures will recall Robert Fogel's (1964, 1979) famous work that showed that railroads in the United States were hardly indispensable since second-best transport—canals, inland rivers, extensive coastlines, and the like—

were abundant. Similar findings emerged for other members of the core, Belgium, Britain, France, and Germany (Hawke 1970; Vamplew 1971; Caron 1983; Fremdling 1983; Laffut 1983). Furthermore, technologies improved on the second-best transport modes in the core as well. However, where regions were fragmented by geography, poorly endowed with inland rivers, and isolated from coastlines, railroads had a spectacular market-integrating impact. Thus, the social savings of the railroads were very big, for example, in Argentina (Summerhill 2001), the Brazilian Southeast (Summerhill 2005), Mexico (Coatsworth 1979, 1981), and Spain (Gómez Mendoza 1982; Herranz-Loncán 2003). Thus, the railroad had a profound impact on integrating domestic commodity markets in much of the periphery and connecting them to the world economy, as illustrated by Porfirian Mexico in the decades up to World War I (Dobado and Marrero 2005).

While the fall in transport costs influencing Asian trade was certainly dramatic, even by the standards of the Atlantic economy, it was not the greatest globalization event affecting the region. Under the persuasion of Commodore Perry's American gunships, Japan signed the Shimoda and Harris ("unequal") treaties and in so doing switched from autarky to free trade in 1858. It is hard to imagine a more dramatic switch in trade policy since Japan's foreign trade quickly rose from nil to 7 percent of national income (Huber 1971). Other Asian nations followed the same liberal path, most forced to do so by colonial dominance or gunboat diplomacy. Thus, following the Opium Wars, China signed a treaty with Britain in 1842, which opened her ports to trade and which set a 5 percent ad valorem tariff limit. Siam avoided China's humiliation by going open and adopting a 3 percent tariff limit in 1855. Korea emerged from its autarkic "Hermit Kingdom" stance about the same time, undergoing market integration with Japan long before colonial status became formalized in 1910 (Brandt 1993; Kang and Cha 1996). India went the way of British free trade in 1846, and Indonesia followed Dutch commercial liberalism. Thus, sharply declining transport costs contributed to commodity price convergence in Asia with no offsetting rise in tariffs; indeed, the midcentury removal of restrictions and embargoes by East Asia on its trade with the core added greatly to those convergence forces.

By the late nineteenth century, transport innovations had eroded both Australia's and Asia's geographic isolation from Europe. Was the same true of Latin America? Before the completion of the Panama Canal in 1914, the Andean economies—Chile, Peru, and Ecuador—were seriously disadvantaged in European and east coast U.S. trade. And prior to the introduction of an effective railroad network, land-locked Bolivia and Paraguay were at an even more serious disadvantage. This was also true of the Mexican interior (Coatsworth 1981), the Argentine interior (Newland 1998), the Colombian interior (Ocampo 1994: 185–8), and elsewhere. Thus, the economic distance to the European core varied considerably depending on Latin American location. In 1842, the cost of moving a ton of goods from England to the capital cities in Latin America (in pounds sterling) was: Buenos Aires and Montevideo 2; Lima 5.12; Santiago 6.58; Caracas 7.76; Mexico City 17.9; Quito 21.3; Sucre or Chuquisca 25.6; and Bogotá 52.9. The range was huge, with the costs to Bogotá, Chuquisca, Mexico City, Quito, and Sucre nine to twenty-seven times that of Buenos Aires and Montevideo, both well placed on either side of the Rio de la Plata (Brading 1969: 243–244).

Furthermore, most of the difference in transport costs from London to Latin America's capital cities was the overland freight from Latin American port to interior capital (Prados 2003). The most populated areas under colonial rule were the highlands. Mexico City, Lima, and the other Andean capital cities were far from accessible harbors, thus increasing transport costs to big foreign markets. In contrast, the Latin American regions bordering on the Atlantic, with long coastlines and good navigable river systems, have always been favored. These include Argentina, Uruguay, Brazil, Cuba, and the other Caribbean islands. These regional economies may have failed for other reasons, but geographic isolation certainly was not one of them: their harbors were located conveniently in relation to the lowlands that were suitable for tropical agriculture, as was the case for sugar, coffee, tobacco, cacao, rubber, and other primary products.

It has been estimated that distance, geography and access to foreign markets explained a third of the world's variation in per capita income as late as 1996 (Redding and Venables 2000; Overman, Redding, and Venables 2001). Not surprisingly, therefore, geographic isolation helped explain much of the economic ranking of the young Latin American republics in 1870, too, with poor countries being the most isolated: Peru, Ecuador, Bolivia, and Paraguay were at the bottom of the poverty pecking order; Colombia and Brazil were in the next level; Cuba and Mexico came next; and Argentina and Uruguay were at the top.[4] Railroads helped unlock the Latin American interior that had been so isolated. For example, between 1870 and 1913, freight rates on overseas routes connecting Uruguay with Europe fell by 0.7 percent per annum, but they fell by 3.1 percent per annum along the railroads penetrating the interior pampas, more than four times as big (Bértola 2000: table 4.1, 102). Railroads were vital in integrating periphery and core markets.

It is also important to note that the impact of the transport revolution on overseas freight rates was unequal along different sea routes. Overseas freight rates fell much less along the southward leg to Latin America than along the northward leg back to Europe, and the fall along the latter does not seem to have been as great as that for Asian and North Atlantic routes (Stemmer 1989: 24). The northward leg was for the bulky Latin American staple exports—including beef, wheat, and guano, the high-volume, low-value primary products whose trade gained so much by the transport revolution. The southward leg was for Latin American imports—including textiles and machines, the high-value, low-volume manufactures whose trade gained much less from the transport revolution. The transport revolution served to erase price differentials between periphery and core much more dramatically for primary products than for manufactures simply because primary products had much bigger price differentials to erase when the transport revolution began in 1820.[5]

World Transport: From Revolutions to Steady State?

This narrative about the world transport revolution is quantified in table 2.2 over the century or so between 1870 and 1990. Note there are four inserts, each offering an estimate of the impact of declining transport costs—restricted to seaborne freight—on the price gap between sending and receiving regions. The representative primary product used in these calculations is grain, and the estimated decline in the freight rate index is applied to the initial production cost

Table 2.2
Global Transport-Cost Changes and Commodity-Price Convergence 1870–1990

1. The Big-Bang Era before World War I		
The Greater Atlantic Economy		
Transport-Cost Declines		
American export routes, deflated freight cost (1869–1871 = 100)	1869/71–1908/10	100 to 55
American east-coast routes, deflated freight cost (1869–1871 = 100)	1869/71–1911/13	100 to 55
Addendum: freight cost/wheat price	*41 to 22.6 or 4.6% pts. per decade*	
British tramp, deflated freight cost (1869–1871 = 100)	1869/71–1911/13	100 to 78
Freight costs as percentage of wheat price	1870–1910	41 to 22.6
Commodity-Price Convergence		
Liverpool-Chicago wheat-price gap (percent)	1870–1912	58 to 16
London-Cincinnati bacon-price gap (percent)	1870–1913	93 to 18
Philadelphia-London pig-iron-price gap (percent)	1870–1913	85 to 19
London-Boston wool-price gap (percent)	1870–1913	59 to 28
London-Buenos Aires hides-price gap (percent)	1870–1913	28 to 9
The Third World		
Transport-Cost Declines		
Rangoon-Europe freight costs as percentage of rice price	1882–1914	74 to 18

Addendum: freight cost/rice price

		18.7% pts. per decade	
Java-Amsterdam sugar freight-cost (1870 = 100)	1870–1914	100 to 45
Nagasaki-Shanghai coal freight-cost (1880 = 100)	1880–1910	100 to 24

Commodity-Price Convergence

Liverpool-Odessa wheat-price gap (percent)	1870–1906	40 to 2
Liverpool vs. Bombay cotton-price gap (percent)	1873–1913	57 to 20
London vs. Calcutta jute-price gap (percent)	1873–1913	35 to 4
London-Rangoon rice-price gap (percent)	1873–1913	93 to 26
Liverpool-Alexandria cotton-price gap (percent)	1837/46–1890/99	63 to 5

2. The Era of Slowdown to Steady State, 1920–1990

Transport-Cost Declines

World Bank deflated ocean-freight-cost index (1920 = 100)	1920–1940	100 to 68
	27.5 to 18.7% or 4.4% pts. per decade	
Addendum: freight cost/wheat price		
Freight costs as percentage of wheat price	1920–1940	27.5 to 18.7
World Bank deflated ocean-freight-cost index (1950 = 100)	1950–1990	100 to 76
	18.7 to 14.2% or 1.1% pts. per decade	
Addendum: freight cost/wheat price		
Freight costs as percentage of wheat price	1950–1990	18.7 to 14.2

Note: Commodity-price gap calculated as the percent by which high-price importing locations exceed low-price exporting locations.

Source: Williamson (2002b: table 1).

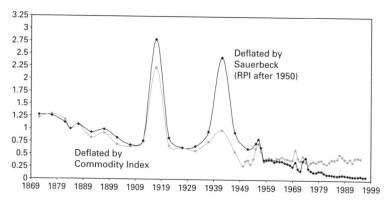

Figure 2.2
Real global freight rate index (1869–1997)
(1884 = 1.00)
Source: Mohammed and Williamson (2004: figure 4).

of grain at the beginning of each period to get an estimate of the percentage points per decade by which the ratio of freight costs to production costs declined. These estimates confirm that the pre–World War I decline in transport costs was most spectacular where it involved the periphery. They also confirm that the prewar decline slowed down during the interwar decades, and fell only modestly after 1950.

This secular trend in global real freight rates is summarized in figure 2.2 using a somewhat different database (Mohammed and Williamson 2004: figure 4), where there are two series plotted: one series, which I strongly prefer, deflates the nominal freight rate index by an index of the prices of the commodities actually transported (Commodity Index); the second series deflates by some GDP deflator that, regrettably, includes services and other nontradables (RPI). According to the preferred index, the period between 1870 and 1914 saw an almost uninterrupted fall in shipping costs relative to the prices of the commodities carried; the war and interwar years were ones of great instability and little downward trend; and the half century since 1950 has been one of stability and no downward trend.

If, then, transport cost trends are measured by overseas freight rates, it is clear that the world transport revolution that took place prior to World War I has moderated greatly since then. However, we do not yet have the evidence to augment this long-run time series to include any of the technological events that may have made harbors more efficient. More importantly, overseas freight rates will not capture any of the technological events that in recent decades have fostered trade in services. Still, my guess is that any analysis of the protrade transport forces at work in the periphery up to 1940 will be well covered by the overseas freight rate trends.

Primary-Product Boom (and Bust) in the Core

Consider the trade booms driven both by the transportation revolution and the primary-product demand boom in the core. The share of Latin American exports in GDP increased by two-and-a-half times from 10 percent in 1850 to 25 percent in 1912 (Bulmer-Thomas 1994: table A.2.1, 439). The increase in the export share between 1870 and 1913 was about the same for Asia, Africa, and the Middle East: it doubled in Asia from 1.7 to 3.4 percent, and it increased by three-and-a-half times in Africa (including Egypt) from 5.8 to 20 percent (Maddison 2002: 127). Still, the growth in world trade was much more dramatic up to 1900 than it was between 1900 and 1913, tracing out a slowdown in world trade growth at the end of the secular boom (Estevadeordal, Frantz, and Taylor 2003). A fading secular boom turned into a secular bust after 1913. Except for Asia, export shares in

GDP fell between 1913 and 1950 in the periphery: by 3 percentage points in Latin America and by 4.9 percentage points in Africa (Maddison 2002: 127).[6]

Although it certainly would be a revealing exercise, it is not my purpose here to sort out exactly how much of the secular trade boom and bust in the periphery was driven by the flow and ebb of transport revolutions worldwide, the flow and ebb of industrial revolutions in the core, or the state of trade policy in the periphery. However, table 2.2 and figure 2.2 document a slowdown in the decline of freight rates in the latter part of the first global century, followed by approximate stability in the interwar years, trends that are certainly correlated with the behavior of trade shares in the periphery. Similarly, while industrial production grew at 2.6 percent per annum in the European core up to 1850, that growth slowed down to 2.5 percent per annum between 1850 and 1913, and then recorded no growth at all up to 1938.[7]

I am hardly the first to note the correlation between the growth of industrial production in the core and export shares in the periphery. Indeed, W. Arthur Lewis stressed this correlation in his Janeway Lectures almost thirty years ago (Lewis 1978), and even then he was summarizing work that he had accumulated over the previous two decades. This is what Lewis had to say:

When the developed countries are expanding, as in the thirty years up to 1913, the developing countries move ahead; when the developed are depressed, as they were for the nearly three decades that included the two world wars, the developing are almost at a standstill . . . We even have a precise measure of the link. World trade in primary products grew about 0.87 times as fast as industrial production in the developed countries between 1883 and 1913 . . . Insofar as exporting primary products is the engine of growth of developing countries, this engine beats rather more slowly than industrial production. (Lewis 1978: 65)

I am sure Lewis would have agreed, however, that it is a mistake to focus solely on the derived primary-product demand coming from industrial growth in the core, and to ignore the trade-creating impact of transport revolutions. They were both at work. In addition, to stress only the best-documented years after 1870, is probably to miss the earlier decades when globalization had its biggest impact in the periphery, and when the terms of trade boom was greatest.

3

World Market Integration and the Periphery Terms of Trade

Commodity Price Convergence and Trade Booms

These transport innovations significantly lowered the cost of moving goods between markets, an event that fostered commodity price convergence and trade between core and periphery. While other forces may have been at work fostering trade, the best measure of the market integration (or globalization) is the behavior of commodity price gaps between export and import markets.

Before I document the remarkable commodity price convergence across the first global century, I want to stress the absence of any such commodity price convergence before. Kevin O'Rourke and I (2002a, 2002b) have shown that there is very little evidence confirming commodity price convergence between Asia and Europe over the three centuries following 1492, while there is plenty of evidence confirming its absence. Consider, for example, the measured price gaps between Amsterdam and Southeast Asia for cloves, coffee, and black pepper from the 1590s onwards, important evidence documenting the presence or absence of world market integration given that spices and pepper combined were 68 percent of Dutch homeward cargoes in the mid-

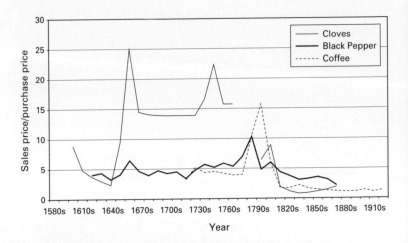

Figure 3.1
Spice and coffee markups: Amsterdam versus Southeast Asia 1580–1939
Source: O'Rourke and Williamson (2002b: figure 4).

seventeenth century (Reid 1993: 288–289). We have clove
price gaps between Amsterdam and Maluku (in the Southeast Asian archipelago), pepper price gaps between Amsterdam and Sumatra (in the Dutch East Indies), and coffee
price gaps between Amsterdam and Java or Sumatra
(Bulbeck, Reid, Tan, and Wu 1998).

Figure 3.1 plots these gaps, measured as the ratio of the
European to the Asian price. There is plenty of evidence of
price convergence for cloves down to the 1640s, but it was
short-lived, since the spread soared to a 350-year high in the
1660s, maintaining that high level during the Dutch East
India Company monopoly up to the 1770s. The clove price
gap fell steeply after the end of the French Wars, and by the
1820s was one-fourteenth of the 1730s level. This narrow
spread was maintained across the nineteenth century. The

pepper price spread showed no trend at all between the 1620s and the 1730s, after which it soared to a 250-year high in the 1790s. By the 1820s, the pepper price spread of the early seventeenth century was recovered, and, once started, the price convergence continued up to the 1880s, when the series ends. While there is some evidence of price convergence for coffee during the half century between the 1730s and the 1780s, everything gained was lost during the French Wars. At the war's end, price convergence came on in a rush, so that the coffee price spread in the 1850s was one-sixth of what it had been in the 1750s, and in the 1930s it was one-thirteenth of what it had been in the 1730s. In all three cases, the story is the same: while substantial price convergence occurred after 1800, little or no price convergence took place before.

Similarly, there is no evidence that Anglo-Indian price convergence took place from the mid-seventeenth to the mid-eighteenth century. There was no decline in price markups for the East India Company's trade in pepper, tea, raw silk, coffee, and indigo, between about 1660 and 1710 (O'Rourke and Williamson 2002b: figure 5). Finally, and perhaps most notably, figure 3.2 shows clearly that there was absolutely no decline in markups on the Anglo-Indian cloth trade (where markups include all trade costs, as well as any East India Company monopoly profits) over the century between 1664 and 1759.

Thus, the trade expansion between 1500 and 1800 appears to have been due to demand and supply growth within the trading continents, not to commodity market integration between them. While there were certainly significant transport improvements on long-distance sea trade over these three centuries, trading monopolies absorbed those rents,

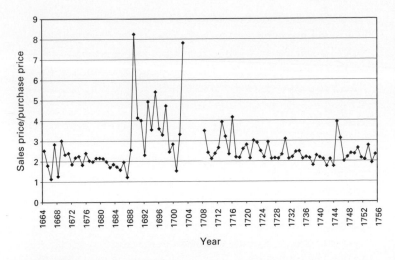

Figure 3.2
Asian textile trade markups: 1664–1759
Source: O'Rourke and Williamson (2002b: figure 6).

not producers and consumers affected by trade. It follows that Euro-Asian and Euro-American trade boomed after Columbus and da Gama in spite of barriers to trade and mercantilist sentiment, not because of some proglobal policies and institutions. In the three centuries before 1800, as much as 65 percent of the European long distance trade expansion can be explained by European income growth, 35 percent by (net) supply expansion in Asia and the Americas, and none of it by declining trade barriers (O'Rourke and Williamson 2002a: 439).

Now consider the spectacular commodity price convergence that followed those three antiglobal centuries between 1500 and 1800, beginning with the Atlantic economy. Liverpool wheat prices still exceeded Chicago wheat prices by a big factor in 1870, 58 percent, but by only 18 and 16 percent in 1895 and 1912, respectively. Overall price convergence was even greater when account is taken of the collapse in price gaps between Midwestern farm gates and Chicago, as well as between Liverpool docks and British inland markets. This price convergence in Anglo-American wheat markets was repeated for other foodstuffs, such as meat, butter, and cheese.

While there was no convergence in London-Cincinnati price differentials for bacon across the 1870s, there was convergence after 1880. Indeed, the price convergence after 1895 was even more dramatic for meat than it had been previously for wheat: price gaps were 93 percent in 1870, still 92 percent in 1895, but only 18 percent in 1913. The price convergence for meat, butter, and cheese was delayed since it had to await the advances in refrigeration made towards the end of the century. Anglo-American price data are also available for many nonagricultural commodities. The Philadelphia-London iron bar price gap fell from 75 percent in 1870 to 21 percent in 1913, the pig iron price gap fell from 85 to 19 percent, and the copper price gap fell from 33 percent to almost zero. The Boston-London hides price gap fell from 28 to 9 percent, and the wool price gap fell from 59 to 28 percent. Finally, the Boston-Manchester cotton textile price gap fell from 14 percent to about zero.

Similar trends can be documented for commodity price gaps between London, on the one hand, and Buenos Aires, Montevideo, and Rio de Janeiro, on the other (Williamson 1999). The Ukraine and the rest of the east European periphery was also part of this worldwide price convergence: wheat price gaps between Odessa and Liverpool of about 40 percent in 1870 had just about evaporated by 1906 (O'Rourke 1997). Commodity price convergence involving the eastern Mediterranean was just as powerful. The price spread on Egyptian cotton between Liverpool and Alexandria plunged off a high plateau after the 1860s. The average percent by which Liverpool price quotes exceeded those in Alexandria was (for the same cotton quality): 1837–1846, 63; 1863–1867, 41; 1882–1889, 15; and 1890–1899, 5 (Issawi 1966: 447–448).

Transport cost declines from interior to port and from port to Europe ensured that Asian export-oriented enclaves also became more integrated into world markets. The raw cotton price spread between Liverpool and Bombay fell from 57 percent in 1873 to 20 percent in 1913, and the jute price spread between London and Calcutta fell from 35 to 4 percent. The same events were taking place even farther east, involving Burma and the rest of Southeast Asia: the rice price spread between London and Rangoon fell from 93 to 26 percent in the four decades prior to 1913. These events had a profound impact on the creation of an Asian market for wheat and rice, as well as a truly global market for all grains (Latham and Neal 1983; Brandt 1985; Kang and Cha 1996). By the end of the century, the state of the monsoon in South Asia had its impact on grain prices quoted in the Chicago exchange.

This narrative is summarized in table 2.2, which also reports the effort to quantify the magnitudes of the transport revolution over the century or so between 1870 and 1990, already discussed previously.

Terms of Trade in the Periphery

So, what did this premodern experience with industrialization in the core and transport revolutions worldwide imply for the terms of trade in the periphery?

When deindustrialization forces are confronted later in these lectures, I will explore the full sweep of terms-of-trade behavior in the periphery starting with the early nineteenth century. There we will see a big boom in the terms of trade everywhere in the periphery up to the 1860s, a more modest increase from the 1860s to the 1890s (although much bigger in Latin America), and a slump thereafter (see figures 5.1, 5.7–5.8, 6.1, 6.2 later). For the present, let us focus on the seventy years from 1870 to 1940.

Table 3.1 is based on terms-of-trade estimates that are averaged over half decades. All of these estimates are constructed from price quotes in home markets, and all are aggregated up using country-specific trade, production, or consumption weights. *Pa* refers to agricultural goods,[1] *Pm* to manufactured goods, *Pexp* to exports, and *Pimp* to imports. Thus, we have annual time series for both the internal terms of trade facing agriculture and the external terms of trade facing each country in the sample. This country-specific evidence is summarized at the regional level in table 3.1. This is only a small sample of periphery economies, but it includes: three from the English-speaking overseas new world—Australia, Canada, and the United States; six from Asia and the Middle East—Burma, Egypt, Japan, Korea, the Punjab, and Siam; and two from Latin America—Argentina and Uruguay. The sample excludes many of the regions and commodities that Lewis caught in his broader net: like Ceylon (tea), Chile (nitrates and copper), Malaysia (rubber and tin), Brazil (coffee and sugar), or sub-Saharan Africa (cocoa and metals). But the central goal of this part of my lectures is to assess the impact of globalization on factor prices and income distribution in the periphery. Only this sample offers the data to make that

Table 3.1
Global *Pa/Pm* and *Pexp/Pimp* Changes on Either Side of World War I (in percent)

Region	(1) Early 1890s to WWI	(2) Early 1870s to WWI	(3) Interwar	(4) Trend Change (3)–(1)
Pa/Pm Changes				
Land-Abundant New World	17.7	−0.2	−14.5	−32.2
Land-Abundant Third World	31.6	40.5	−9.1	−40.7
Average Land-Abundant Countries	27.0	24.2	−11.2	−38.2
Land-Scarce Third World	22.7	14.4	−3.3	−26.0
Land-Scarce Europe	9.0	20.5	−5.6	−14.6
Average Land-Scarce Countries	12.0	19.7	−4.9	−16.9
Pexp/Pimp Changes				
Land-Abundant New World	10.7	25.7	7.8	−2.9
Land-Abundant Third World	21.1	48.5	−4.0	−25.1
Average Land-Abundant Countries	17.6	37.1	0.4	−17.2
Land-Scarce Third World	−18.4	9.5	−23.1	−4.7
Land-Scarce Europe	0.9	1.9	11.1	10.2
Average Land-Scarce Countries	−3.9	3.4	0.8	4.7

Source: Williamson (2002b, table 2). Land-Abundant New World = Australia, Canada, and United States; Land-Abundant Third World = Argentina, Burma, Egypt, Punjab, Uruguay, and Thailand; Land-Scarce Third World = Japan, Korea, and Taiwan; Land-Scarce Europe = Great Britain, Denmark, Ireland, Sweden, France, Germany, and Spain.

connection. Later in these lectures I use a far bigger sample to explore the terms-of-trade connection with GDP per capita and its growth.

So, what should we expect to find? If commodity price convergence had been the only force at work up to World War I, *Pexp/Pimp* should have improved for all countries: after all, commodity price convergence should have raised the price of exportables and lowered the price of importables for practically all trading partners; at the very least, it cannot have lowered the price of exportables or raised the price of importables for any country, thus causing a deterioration in its external terms of trade. And if commodity price convergence had been the only force at work up to World War I, *Pa/Pm* should also have improved for all land (and resource) abundant economies, which exported agricultural goods, while it should have deteriorated for all land (and resource) scarce economies, which exported manufactures. These relative price shocks should also have been bigger in the periphery where the transport revolution seems to have been bigger. All of these predictions are qualified by the if: after all, there were world supply and demand forces at work that also influenced relative price trends. Still, the qualified predictions are confirmed for the first global century (which says a great deal about the magnitude of commodity price convergence during those years).

First, the terms of trade improved for all trading regions except one, and the exception comes only late in the period. Thus, *Pexp/Pimp* rose everywhere from the early 1870s to World War I, and it rose everywhere from the early 1890s to World War I, except East Asia (table 3.1). Commodity price convergence seems to have benefited all trading participants during the first global century, and this force dominated other world market forces in almost all times and places.

Second, Pa/Pm rose more in the land abundant periphery than in the land scarce core. From the early 1870s to World War I, Pa/Pm increased by 20.5 percent in Europe and by 14.4 percent in East Asia, for an average of 19.7 percent in these two land-scarce areas.[2] The figures are bigger for the poorer parts of the land-abundant periphery. Thus, Pa/Pm increased by 40.5 percent in the land abundant Third World over the four decades following the 1870s. While it did not increase at all in the New World, the average increase for the two land-abundant regions was 24.2 percent. From the early 1890s to World War I, the figure is 12 percent for all land-scarce regions and 27 percent for all land-abundant regions. During the first global century, Pa/Pm rose by more in the land- and resource-abundant parts of the periphery than in the labor- and capital-abundant parts of the core.

Third, $Pexp/Pimp$ and Pa/Pm both rose by more in land abundant regions than in land scarce regions. From the early 1890s to World War I, Pa/Pm rose by 27 and 12 percent in land-abundant and land-scarce countries, respectively, while $Pexp/Pimp$ recorded a 17.6 percent rise and a 3.9 percent fall. From the early 1870s to World War I, Pa/Pm rose by 24.2 and 19.7 percent in land-abundant and land-scarce countries, respectively, while $Pexp/Pimp$ rose by 37.1 and 3.4 percent. The land- and resource-abundant parts of the world (whether core or periphery) enjoyed far more favorable price shocks prior to World War I than did the resource-scarce parts of the world (whether core or periphery).

Fourth, $Pexp/Pimp$ and Pa/Pm both rose by more in the land-abundant Third World than in the land-abundant New World. Again, table 3.1 illustrates the point: Pa/Pm rose by 40.5 percent in the land-abundant Third World between the early 1870s and World War I compared with no rise at all in the land-abundant New World.[3] The figures for *Pexp/Pimp* are 48.5 and 25.7 percent. Between the early 1890s and World War I, *Pa/Pm* rose by 31.6 percent in the land-abundant Third World compared with 17.7 percent in the land-abundant New World. The comparative figures for *Pexp/Pimp* are 21.1 and 10.7 percent. Commodity price convergence in the first global century caused a predictable convergence in *Pa/Pm* between land-scarce and land-abundant countries the world around, but the boom in *Pa/Pm* and *Pexp/Pimp* in the land-abundant parts of Latin America, the eastern Mediterranean, and Asia was bigger than in North America and Australasia.

Fifth, *Pa/Pm* rose worldwide during the first global century. Thus, the predictions of the classical economists appear to be borne out: rapid productivity advance in manufacturing, and inelastic factor supplies in resource-constrained primary-product sectors, both served to generate a fall in the relative price of manufactures and a rise in the relative price of primary products. We should note, however, that the rise in *Pa/Pm* and *Pexp/Pimp* facing the land-abundant Third World was less dramatic after the 1890s than before, a slowdown that will be seen again in chapter 6 with a much larger sample.

Relative price trends underwent a dramatic reversal after World War I, partly because the transport revolution had come to a halt, partly because the core retreated towards autarky, and partly because of a retardation in world growth led by a slowdown in the industrial core.[4] The first should have halted commodity price convergence, the second should have reversed it, and the third should have taken the steam out of the primary-product boom everywhere. Thus, *Pa/Pm* collapsed in all regions after World War I, although it collapsed by more in land-abundant regions, events that provoked Raúl Prebisch (1950), Hans Singer (1950), Ragnar Nurkse (1953, 1959), Gunnar Myrdal (1957), and William Arthur Lewis (1970, 1978) to infer that the primary-product boom was over and that an epoch of deterioration had set in, events that they thought warranted pro-industry intervention in the periphery. The change in the relative price environment facing primary-product exporters in the periphery was spectacular. In the land-abundant Third World (including Argentina and Uruguay), the difference between the interwar fall in Pa/Pm (–9.1 percent) and the prewar rise (31.6 percent) implied a price-trend reversal of 40.7 percentage points, a very big trend switch for a relative price. In the land-abundant New World (excluding Argentina and Uruguay), the price-trend reversal was 32.2 percentage points, not as big as in the land-abundant Third World, but very big nonetheless. The Pa/Pm trend switch was smaller for land-scarce regions, especially Europe, and this was even more true for its external terms of trade. The $Pexp/Pimp$ trend reversal was the following: land-scarce East Asia –4.7 percent; land-abundant New World (excluding Argentina and Uruguay) –2.9 percent; and land-abundant Third World (including Argentina and Uruguay) –25.1 percent. There was no such $Pexp/Pimp$ trend reversal in Europe since there it rose 10.2 percent.

From where Prebisch and Singer were standing in 1950, it must have looked like the long primary-product boom was over. Indeed, they were observing only the last forty years of a much longer secular boom and bust. If the evidence documenting the full 1820–1940 cycle had been available to them in 1950, no doubt they would have been even more impressed by the extent to which global conditions facing the periphery had changed.

4

Relative Factor Price Convergence, Absolute Factor Price Divergence, and Income Distribution

Global Relative Factor Price Convergence: Theory

What was the effect of industrialization in the core and market integration worldwide on the periphery before 1940? Lewis (1970) pioneered the exploration of this question, looking at factor market responses in primary-product–exporting economies. He composed a long shopping list of effects including the following three: the response of international capital flows;[1] the response of international labor migrations and land settlement;[2] and the impact of the price shocks on deindustrialization everywhere around the periphery, as primary-product export sectors boomed and import-competing manufacturing, like textiles, slumped. The Lewis shopping list also included the impact of the price shocks on income distribution.

This chapter examines the impact on income distribution in the periphery by focusing on factor prices, specifically on the returns to labor relative to land, or what I call the wage-rental ratio.[3] The economist reading this should be warned about my rhetoric since the wage-rental ratio label used here certainly does not refer to the returns to capital relative to labor's wage. Indeed, a well-integrated world capital market insured that risk-adjusted financial capital costs were pretty much equated the world around (Obstfeld and Taylor 2003). Thus, while capital was mobile internationally, labor and land were not. Furthermore, the distribution of income in the nineteenth century periphery was determined just as the classical economists modeled it, namely, by the relative shares of rents and wages in national income. To assess the distribution impact of core industrialization and world commodity market integration on the periphery, I therefore quite naturally focus on labor and land, and the wage-rental ratio. The modern literature, in contrast, focuses on wages by skill and earnings distributions. In the premodern periphery, skills were not a critical factor of production and thus were only marginally relevant to income distributions.

Ever since Eli Heckscher and Bertil Ohlin wrote about the problem almost a century ago (Flam and Flanders 1991), commodity price convergence has been associated with relative factor price convergence. That is, if Pa/Pm converges between trading partners, the wage-rental ratio, w/r, should also converge: w/r should fall in the land-abundant and labor-scarce country (since the export boom raises the relative demand for land) and it should rise in the labor-abundant and land-scarce country (since the export boom raises the relative demand for labor). Since land was held by the favored few, the pre–World War I commodity price convergence implied lesser inequality in land-scarce economies like those in western Europe and East Asia, where land rents (and land values) fell, wages rose, and w/r rose even further.

Where industrialization had not yet taken hold, the pre–World War I commodity price convergence induced a rise in land (and, more generally, resource) rents, a fall in wages, and an even greater fall in w/r for resource-abundant economies, implying greater inequality in Southeast Asia, the Southern Cone, Egypt, and the Punjab, especially in these poor agrarian societies where the ownership of land dictated the ownership of wealth.[4] Furthermore, it appears that globalization served to increase the concentration of land holdings in many regions, like Southeast Asia, thus adding even more to the inequality trends. That is, small holders moving to cash crops accumulated debt (aided by an integrated world capital market) to finance the increased use of purchased inputs, more extensive irrigation systems, and better transportation, all of which was essential to supply booming world markets. It also exposed them to greater price volatility, and default during slumps converted many of these small holders into tenants or into "proletarianized" wage labor on large estates. Thus, cash tenancy on rice-producing land rose in Burma from 25 to 58 percent between the 1900s and 1930s, and similar trends took place in Cochinchina, Assam, and Tonkin (Steinberg 1987). The move to large sugar plantations in the Philippines had the same impact on land concentration there as well (Corpuz 1997), although these forces did not have the same impact in Malaysia and Siam (Steinberg 1987). I will have much more to say about the role of price volatility in this process in chapter 6.

Of course, commodity price convergence was not the only force contributing to a rise in the periphery's terms of trade and, I assume, to a change in wage-rental ratios and income distributions. These distributional forces were strengthened by the strong demand for primary products in industrial markets. They were also strengthened by south–south labor migrations within the periphery, labor-scarce Africa, Latin America, and Southeast Asia absorbing immigrants from labor-abundant China and India (Hatton and Williamson 2005: chapter 7). In any case, what went up, eventually came down: when the secular terms-of-trade boom faded and turned in to a bust somewhere between the beginning of the 1890s and the end of World War I, the relative factor price and distribution trends should also have faded and turned around, ceteris paribus.

My central concern, then, is the connection between the terms of trade and the wage-rental ratio. Later, I document pre-1940 w/r evidence, but first we need to elaborate a bit on the economics. The relevant theory can be found in the work of Max Corden and Fred Gruen (1970), Michael Mussa (1979), and Douglas Irwin (1999), as well as what is known as the magnification effect first identified by Ronald Jones (1979). The models are simple, but they isolate what should be important. An increase in the price of the labor-intensive manufactured good (Pm) shifts its isoprice curve outwards, wages rise, and labor is pulled off the land to satisfy new employment demands in manufacturing. Land rents fall as agricultural labor migrates to manufacturing, leaving land-lords with less labor to cultivate and harvest. The rental-wage (r/w) ratio falls even more since wages have risen. Furthermore, these models yield what is known as a magnification effect, to the extent that the rise in w exceeds the rise in Pm. In contrast, if the price of primary products (here called agriculture for short, and thus Pa for its price) rises, the isoprice curve for primary products shifts outwards, land (and other resource) rents rise, and the rental-wage ratio rises still more. In this example where favorable price shocks are experienced by the country specializing in agri-culture, there is a magnification effect since the rise in rents exceeds the rise in Pa. By symmetry, when Pa/Pm falls, the wage-rental ratio rises, again by a magnification effect.

How big is the magnification effect? In his classic paper on the specific-factor model, Jones (1979) showed exactly what determines the size of the effect. Suppose the agricultural sector uses mobile labor, earning the wage, w, as before, and sector-specific land, earning the rent, r, as before. Suppose further that the manufacturing sector uses mobile labor and sector-specific capital, the latter earning an interest rate i. Now, introduce a shock to this primary-product–exporting economy by raising its terms of trade, Pa/Pm. It must follow that

$$r^* > Pa^* > w^* > Pm^* > i^*,$$

where, once again, "$*$" refers to rates of change. The inequality states that changes in the returns to the sector-specific factors (land and capital) are more pronounced than the return to the mobile factor (labor), a formal result that makes good intuitive sense: after all, while a mobile factor can emigrate from a sector absorbing a bad price shock, an immobile sector-specific factor (such as arable land or mineral resources) cannot. Furthermore, the rental-wage ratio responds as

$$(r^* - w^*) = \Delta(Pa^* - Pm^*)$$

where $\Delta > 1$ denotes the magnification effect. This magnification effect ought to vary from country to country, depending on the size of its primary-product–producing sector and the character of technologies in all sectors. Thus, globalization shocks can have different effects on wage-rental ratios depending on their size and the structure of the economy in question, but the expectation is that $\Delta > 1$ everywhere.

Changes in the land-labor ratio can be treated in much the same way. The rental-wage ratio responds to changes in the endowment ratio as

$$(r^* - w^*) = \mu(L^* - D^*)$$

where L is labor, D is land, and μ denotes the economy-wide response of relative factor prices to changes in the land-labor ratio. The response, μ, is conditioned by the composite of sectoral substitution elasticities, sectoral factor income shares and initial factor distributions between sectors; and, in contrast with Δ, theory does not tell us more than simply that $\mu > 0$. Even if technologies were identical across countries, the size of μ would still vary according to comparative advantage, specialization and, thus, output mix.

These are the essentials that must have been driving relative factor prices, and thus income distribution, in the periphery before 1940. However, in the core (perhaps including Japan), capital-deepening and rapid productivity advance must be added to include the effects of industrialization as it pulls labor off the land and raises the wage-rental ratio, forces that the literature has already identified as important (O'Rourke, Taylor, and Williamson 1996; O'Rourke and Williamson 2005).

Global Relative Factor Price Convergence: The Historical Facts

So much for theory. What about the facts?

The prices of exportables boomed in the primary product-specializing countries up to 1914, or at least in our sample. Price trends reversed thereafter. Thus, the relative rewards to land and labor should have moved in very different directions on either side of World War I. Exactly how they were affected should have depended, of course, on whether the abundant factor was land or labor. Consider the canonical

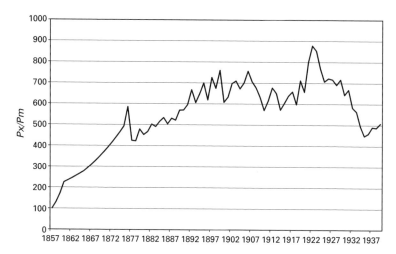

Figure 4.1
Terms of trade for Japan 1857–1939 (1857 = 100)

land scarce and labor abundant case, Japan. When Japan was forced to emerge from isolation after 1858, prices of its labor-intensive exportables soared, rising towards world market levels, while prices of its land- and capital-intensive importables collapsed, falling towards world market levels. One researcher estimated that, as a consequence, the terms of trade rose by a factor of 3.5 over the fifteen late Tokugawa and early Meiji years following 1858 (Huber 1971), while another thought the multiple was 4.9 (Yasuba 1996). These were massive and permanent relative price shocks. Just how permanent can be seen in figure 4.1: not only did Japan's terms of trade increase almost five times after the country opened to trade, but it continued to increased still further up to the 1890s.[5] The Heckscher-Ohlin model predicts what the income distribution response should have been in preindustrial Japan: the abundant factor (labor) should have

flourished while the scarce factor (land) should have lan-
guished after 1858. Did they?

The available factor price evidence for Japan in midcentury is, unfortunately, very limited: data documenting
trends in land rents or land values are not available until
1885, long after Japan's leap to openness had taken place.
But we do have some crude evidence, and it seems
to confirm the Heckscher and Ohlin hypothesis. Angus
Maddison (1995: 196) estimates that Japan's real GDP per
capita increased by only 5.3 percent between 1820 and 1870
(total, not per annum). Assume that all of that modest
increase took place between 1850 and 1870, an unlikely
event that argues against the thesis. Some time ago,
J. Richard Huber (1971) estimated that the real wage for
unskilled workers in Osaka and Tokyo increased by 67
percent during this period. True, this huge measured
increase is much bigger than the real wage growth others
have estimated more recently; in my data, for example, I
have to go back to the late 1830s to find a real wage increase
between then and 1870 anything like that estimated by
Huber (about 63 percent: Williamson 2000), while more
recently others have documented even smaller increases
(Bassino and Ma 2004: 9). Nevertheless, consider the impli-
cation of Huber's estimates: the nominal wage of unskilled
labor, the abundant factor, increased by 43 percent relative
to average nominal income in Japan. Under plausible
assumptions,[6] this example implies that nominal land rents
fell by more than 80 percent. The example also implies that
Japan's wage-rental ratio rose by more than 7.3 times (from
1.0 to 1.67/0.20). This is exactly what one would have predicted when a technologically quiescent economy is hit with
a huge price shock that favors the exportable and disfavors

the importable: the wage-rental ratio should have soared in Japan, with obvious distributional (and, one supposes, political) implications.

A rise in the wage-rental ratio of 7.3 times may seem enormous, but remember the magnification effect discussed in the previous section where I invoked a 3×2 model. To make things simpler here, I use a 2×2 model just to get a feel for historical plausibility. As before, let Pm be the price of labor-intensive manufacturing exportables, Pa the price of land-intensive importables, w the wage rate facing unskilled labor, r the rent on a hectare of rice paddy or other farmland, and $0 < \theta_{rj} = (1 - \theta_{wj}) < 1$ the share of factor payments in sector j going to land rents. Land is far more important in agriculture than manufacturing, so $1/(\theta_{ra} - \theta_{rm}) > 1$, and thus the impact of a relative price shock $(Pm^* - Pa^*)$ has a magnification effect on relative factor prices $(w^* - r^*)$:

$$(Pm^* - Pa^*)/(\theta_{ra} - \theta_{rm}) = (w^* - r^*).$$

If the land share was about 0.4 in agriculture[7] and very small in manufacturing, the magnification effect would be close to 2.5. Thus, a rise in Pm/Pa by 3.5 times could easily have induced a rise in w/r by 7.3 times.

Of course, these are only informed guesses for premodern Japan, but table 4.1 reports more concrete estimates for those countries and time periods which can be documented. Wage-rental ratio trends can be constructed for Japan starting 1885, Korea starting 1909, and Taiwan starting 1904. In contrast with the Punjab after 1873 or Japan after 1858, the early twentieth century was not a period of technological quiescence in East Asian agriculture. Instead, the region was undergoing land-saving and labor-using innovation

Table 4.1
Wage/Rental Ratio Trends in the Third World, 1870–1939 (1911 = 100)

Period	Land-Abundant						Land-Scarce		
	Argentina	Uruguay	Burma	Siam	Egypt	The Punjab	Japan	Korea	Taiwan
1870–1874		1112.5		4699.1		196.7			
1875–1879		891.3		3908.7	174.3	198.5			
1880–1884	580.4	728.3		3108.1	276.6	147.2			
1885–1889	337.1	400.2		2331.6	541.9	150.8	79.9		
1890–1894	364.7	377.2	190.9	1350.8	407.5	108.7	68.6		
1895–1899	311.1	303.6	189.9	301.3	160.1	92.0	91.3		
1900–1904	289.8	233.0	186.8	173.0	166.7	99.8	96.1		68.1
1905–1909	135.2	167.8	139.4	57.2	64.4	92.4	110.4	102.8	85.2
1910–1914	84.0	117.9	106.9	109.8	79.8	80.1	107.5	121.9	96.6
1915–1919	53.6	120.8	164.7	202.1	83.5	82.5	104.9	109.4	111.2
1920–1924	53.1	150.3	113.6	157.9	124.3	81.1	166.1	217.4	140.0
1925–1929	51.0	150.2		114.9	120.8	72.6	202.4	209.2	134.8
1930–1934	58.4	174.3		113.1	116.2	50.4	229.5	194.0	130.7
1935–1939	59.5	213.5		121.6	91.0	33.2	149.9	215.4	123.6

Source: Williamson (2002b: table 3).

(Hayami and Ruttan 1971: chapters 6 and 7), forces that should have served by themselves to raise the wage-rental ratio. It was also a period of early industrialization, at least in Japan and the Shanghai region (Ma 2004), which pulled labor off the farm (Brandt 1985), another force serving to raise the wage-rental ratio. The period after 1910–1914 was, as we have seen, also one of unfavorable farm price shocks (Kimura 1993; Kang and Cha 1996), an additional force serving to raise the wage-rental ratio. In short, we might expect that East Asian wage-rental ratio trends, initiated by globalization forces in the mid-nineteenth century, to have continued into the twentieth century. That is exactly what table 4.1 shows: East Asian wage-rental ratios surged up to the 1920s and 1930s. Land scarce Europe experienced the same surge in wage-rental ratios during the so-called grain invasion after the 1870s, at least where trade policy remained liberal (O'Rourke, Taylor, and Williamson 1996). Furthermore, the magnitudes were pretty similar. Over the fifteen years between 1910–1914 and 1925–1929, the average increase in the wage-rental ratio for Japan, Korea, and Taiwan combined was about 67 percent (table 4.1). Over the fifteen years between 1890–1904 and 1910–1914, the average increase in the wage-rental ratio for Britain, Ireland, Denmark, and Sweden combined was about 50 percent (table 4.2). It might also be relevant to add that politically powerful landed interests were able to secure some protection from these globalization forces in continental Europe by imposing tariffs on grain imports (Rogowski 1989; O'Rourke 1997; Williamson 1997), so that the wage-rental ratio rose only about a third as fast in the average of protectionist France, Germany, and Spain compared with the open four of Britain, Ireland, Denmark, and Sweden. Japan achieved much the same result with import restrictions on rice (Brandt 1993).

Table 4.2
Wage/Rental Ratio Trends in Europe and the New World, 1870–1939 (1911 = 100)

| | Land-Abundant | | | Land-Scarce | | | | | | |
Period	Australia	Canada	United States	Britain	Denmark	France	Germany	Ireland	Spain	Sweden
1870–1874	416.2		233.6	56.6	44.8	63.5	84.4		51.3	42.7
1875–1879	253.0		195.0	61.4	43.5	62.9	80.0	62.2	55.8	43.7
1880–1884	239.1		188.3	64.9	44.8	67.3	82.3	72.7	58.6	50.7
1885–1889	216.3		182.1	73.1	56.6	73.8	86.0	86.4	73.0	57.8
1890–1894	136.2		173.5	79.1	66.7	80.4	98.0	102.7	81.8	65.3
1895–1899	147.7		175.0	87.3	87.9	91.8	108.2	122.1	85.5	78.6
1900–1904	130.0	81.4	172.4	91.4	103.8	103.2	107.6	111.2	74.9	87.9
1905–1909	97.9	93.4	132.7	98.1	99.7	106.4	104.6	101.7	85.7	92.5
1910–1914	100.6	95.6	101.1	102.7	100.0	99.8	100.2	94.1	86.4	99.1
1915–1919	111.0	134.3	124.7	153.1		123.7		79.7	52.5	143.4
1920–1924	137.2	146.5	122.4	197.6		156.5		105.7	38.8	136.5
1925–1929	115.1	236.4	160.1	167.6		117.1		168.6	38.7	116.3
1930–1934	98.3	219.2	165.2	190.3		133.1		192.3	39.1	135.1
1935–1939	110.5	225.1	240.1	206.5		168.2		227.8		

Source: Williamson (2002b: table 4).

In contrast with land-scarce East Asia and Europe, the Punjab appears to have been relatively land abundant, a characterization that is confirmed by the fact that agricultural exports from the Punjab to Europe boomed after the early 1870s, while irrigation investment, immigration, and new settlement made it behave like a frontier region.[8] Globalization should have had the opposite effect on the wage-rental ratio in land-abundant Punjab compared with land-scarce East Asia: it should have fallen, and fall it did. Between 1875–1879 and 1910–1914, the wage-rental ratio in the Punjab fell by 60 percent. The Punjab's wage-rental ratio experience was not so different from that of the Southern Cone and other land abundant parts of the New World. Between 1870–1874 and 1910–1914, the wage-rental ratio fell by 69 percent in the combined pair of Australia and the United States (table 4.2),[9] and between 1880–1884 and 1910–1914 it fell by 85 percent in the combined pair of Argentina and Uruguay (table 4.1). Egypt, riding a cotton boom, conformed to these relative factor price trends: the Egyptian wage-rental ratio fell by 54 percent from the late 1870s to 1910–1914, and by 85 percent from the late 1880s onwards (table 4.1).

The recorded decline in wage-rental ratios in the land-abundant Southern Cone, the Punjab, and Egypt prior to World War I is simply enormous. When compared with the upward surge in wage-rental ratios in land-scarce Europe and East Asia, these trends imply very powerful global relative factor price convergence. But they were even more powerful in land-abundant, labor-scarce, and rice-exporting Southeast Asia: pre-1914 globalization price shocks appear to have lowered the wage-rental ratio in both Burma and Siam, and the decline was huge. The wage-rental ratio fell by 44 percent in Burma over the twenty years between

1890–1894 and 1910–1914. In Siam, it fell by 92 percent between 1890–1894 and 1910–1914, and by an even bigger 98 percent between 1870–1874 and 1910–1914. These are even steeper declines than those recorded in other land-abundant areas such as the Southern Cone, Australia, or North America. These trends had obvious inequality implications in resource-abundant regions as landed interests gained dramatically relative to labor. As I pointed out previously, globalization also served to increase the concentration of land holdings in much of Southeast Asia due to rising small holder indebtedness as they shifted from subsistence to commercial export crops and exposed themselves to greater price volatility associated with many of those crops, resulting in subsequent default for the poorly insured. Small holders evolved in to tenant or wage labor on large estates, inducing more land and wealth concentration, and even more income inequality as a consequence.

We know that relative factor price convergence took place in the Atlantic economy over the four decades or so following 1870 (O'Rourke, Taylor, and Williamson 1996). These factor-price convergence trends are reproduced in table 4.2, where new evidence for the interwar period and new evidence for Uruguay (table 4.1) join revisions of the rest, yielding pre-1940 data for five land-abundant overseas settlements—Argentina, Australia, Canada, Uruguay, and the United States; four land-scarce European countries that pretty much stuck to free trade—Denmark (data only to 1913), Great Britain, Ireland, and Sweden (data only to 1930); and three land-scarce European countries that raised tariffs to help fend off the winds of competition—France, Germany (data only to 1913), and Spain (data only to 1934). Land-scarce European countries that raised tariffs to fend off foreign agricultural competition underwent a less dramatic increase in their wage-rental ratio, but wage-rental ratios still rose everywhere in Europe.

What happened after 1914 when so many countries in the Atlantic economy retreated behind tariff walls, quotas, and other nontariff barriers, underwent competitive devaluations, restricted across-border migrations, and used other devices to retreat towards autarky? Relative factor price convergence ceased, and in many cases divergence set in. The pre-1914 decline in the wage-rental ratio turned around in land-abundant Australia, Canada, and the United States and rose to 1935–1939. The same was true of land-abundant Argentina, Uruguay, Egypt, Burma, and Siam (although the Punjab appears to have been an exception to the rule). The wage-rental ratio surge in land scarce Europe and East Asia did not, however, reverse after 1914, but the previous rate of rise does appear to have slowed down.

The relative factor-price-convergence theorem seems to have been alive and well in the world economy before the modern era. During the proglobal decades before World War I, commodity price and relative factor price convergence took place worldwide: the wage-rental ratio rose in labor-abundant and land-scarce trading partners while it fell in land-abundant and labor-scarce trading partners, and the Asian and Middle Eastern periphery joined the European core (and its overseas settlements) in those trends. During the antiglobal decades after World War I, global relative factor price convergence halted.

Global Relative Factor Price Convergence: Some Econometrics

Can we make the empirical connection between commodity price convergence and relative factor price convergence more precise? The theory reviewed earlier suggests four forces that might account for the wage-rental trends documented in tables 4.1 and 4.2. First, there are the forces of globalization and world markets, measured here by changes in the relative price of agricultural goods, Pa/Pm. Theory argues that the impact of Pa/Pm should vary across economies, the size of the impact correlated negatively with the level of development and positively with the size of the agricultural sector. To accommodate this possibility, I estimate independently these country-specific forces within four regional groups: the land-abundant New World; land-scarce Europe; the land-scarce Third World; and the land-abundant Third World. Second, trends in the land-labor ratio should matter, and they exhibit considerable variety over time and space. Third, capital-deepening in the nonfarm sector should draw labor off the land and raise the wage-rental ratio. Fourth, while factor-saving technological change was apparently very weak in the preindustrial Third World, we know it was very strong in industrializing Europe, North America, Australia, and Japan. Earlier work on the greater Atlantic economy has shown that the land-saving technological change, which characterized land-scarce Europe, made a powerful contribution to rising wage-rental ratios there, and it also showed that the labor-saving technological change, which characterized labor scarce North America and Australia, made a powerful contribution to falling wage-rental ratios there (O'Rourke, Taylor, and Williamson 1996: table 3; O'Rourke and Williamson 1999; Williamson 2002b).

Unfortunately, causality problems and inadequate data complicate the empirical assessment. Pre-1940 capital stock data are missing for most of the periphery, so we must rely on proxies for the absent capital-labor ratios. Missing, too, are measures of total factor productivity growth. In contrast, they are available for the better-documented greater Atlantic economy. To make possible comparisons between the Third World and the Atlantic economy, I have replaced the productivity and capital-labor variables with a popular proxy, the share of the population urban.[10] Empirical work is made even more challenging by problems of causality. While an exogenous rise in the land-labor ratio will raise the wage-rental ratio, ceteris paribus, can we be sure that late nineteenth-century factor endowments were exogenous? High and rising wage-rental ratios probably generated a factor supply response. The land-labor ratio may have declined as positive Malthusian forces associated with labor scarcity encouraged early marriage, high fertility in marriage, and high child survival rates. Labor scarcity also encouraged across-border migration[11] and thus an even greater and quicker decline in the land-labor ratio. Alternatively, high and rising wage-rental ratios may have fostered frontier settlement by land-hungry labor, a response that has received considerable theoretical and empirical attention in the literature (Findlay 1995; O'Rourke and Williamson 1999: chapter 7; Hatton and Williamson 1998, 2005: chapter 4). So, what should we expect? A positive or a negative sign on land-labor ratios in the reduced-form regressions explaining wage-rental ratios? We cannot be sure until causality issues are resolved, and these might well differ between regions. Since I believe that these questions are far too important to await the collection of even more data and the discovery of clever instruments, I report what I have found from ordinary least squares.

Table 4.3 reports OLS with fixed effects for all nineteen countries, and for each of the four regions separately: land-abundant New World (29 percent of the sample)—

Table 4.3
OLS Estimation with Fixed Effects, 1870–1940
Dependent Variable: Wage/Rental Ratio

Variables	All Countries	New World	Europe	Asia: Land-Abundant	Asia: Land-Scarce
Pa/Pm	−0.62*	−0.58*	−0.44*	−1.28*	−0.23***
	(0.093)	(0.121)	(0.098)	(0.251)	(0.138)
Land/Labor	−0.22**	0.32*	−0.87*	−3.94*	−0.89***
	(0.088)	(0.086)	(0.088)	(0.639)	(0.473)
Urbanization	0.22*	−0.95*	0.50*	−0.43	0.60*
	(0.072)	(0.102)	(0.052)	(0.501)	(0.116)
Constant	8.67*	4.42*	11.14*	27.36*	10.82*
	(0.556)	(0.670)	(0.486)	(2.617)	(2.111)
Observations	1055	308	404	226	117
Adjusted R^2	0.40	0.44	0.64	0.44	0.57
Significance level	—	5%	1%	1%	1%

Notes: (*): significant at 1%, (**): significant at 5%, (***): significant at 10%. The first row indicates the coefficient estimates and the second row the standard deviation (in parenthesis). All variables are in natural logarithms, and the estimations are OLS with fixed effects. New World: Argentina, Australia, Canada, Uruguay, and the United States; Europe: Great Britain, Denmark, France, Germany, Ireland, Spain, and Sweden; Land-Abundant Asia: Burma, Egypt, the Punjab, and Thailand; Land-Scarce Asia: Japan, Korea, and Taiwan.

Argentina, Australia, Canada, Uruguay, and the United States; land-scarce Europe (38 percent of the sample)—Great Britain, Denmark, France, Germany, Ireland, Spain, and Sweden; land-abundant Asia and the Middle East (22 percent of the sample)—Burma, Egypt, the Punjab, and Thailand; and land-scarce Asia (11 percent of the sample)—Japan, Korea, and Taiwan. Country fixed-effect estimation is required since the *Pa/Pm* series, the *w/r* series and the land-labor endowment series are all indexed at 1911, so cross-country variance in any year has no meaning. All variables are in natural logarithms.

As theory predicts, the impact of Pa/Pm is everywhere negative and significant: a boom in the relative price of agricultural goods raised the rent on land relative to the wage for labor; a slump had the opposite effect. Furthermore, the impact was far bigger in the land-abundant regions where agriculture played a far bigger role: the New World coefficient on Pa/Pm is 1.3 times bigger than that for Europe; and the coefficient for land-abundant Asia is 5.6 times that for land scarce Asia. Thus, we have now confirmed two reasons why globalization had such a big impact on income distribution in the Middle East, South Asia, and Southeast Asia, and such a small impact in Europe: the Pa/Pm shocks and their impact multipliers were both smaller in Europe. The surprise, however, is that the oft-cited "magnification effect" is absent from table 4.3 except for land-abundant Asia: that is, only for land-abundant Asia is the absolute value of the coefficient in the first row of the table greater than unity (–1.28). The modified regression equations in table 4.4 reported below show somewhat higher coefficients on Pa/Pm, but even there the magnification effect is shown to have been present in less than half of the pre-1940 global economy.

Next, consider the urbanization proxy. To the extent that an increase in the proxy serves to capture capital-deepening and industrial total factor productivity advance, rising urbanization rates should have been associated with the strong pull of labor off the land, and thus with rising wage-rental ratios. Urbanization should have a positive coefficient, at least where industrial revolutionary events were

Table 4.4
Specific Group Estimations, OLS with Fixed Effects, 1870–1940
Dependent Variable: Wage/Rental Ratio

New World		Europe		Asia: Land-Abundant		Asia: Land-Scarce	
Variables	Coefficients	Variables	Coefficients	Variables	Coefficients	Variables	Coefficients
Pa/Pm	-0.67* (0.073)	$Pa/Pm \times$ GB	-1.13* (0.356)	Pa/Pm	-1.33* (0.214)	Pa/Pm	-0.37* (0.136)
Land/Labor	0.85* (0.081)	$Pa/Pm \times$ DEN	-3.94* (0.803)	Land/Labor	-4.80* (0.567)	Land/Labor $\times$ TAI	2.87** (1.179)
Urb $\times$ ARG	-4.94* (0.210)	$Pa/Pm \times$ SWE	0.99* (0.256)	Urb $\times$ EGY	-6.20* (0.952)	Land/Labor $\times$ KOR	6.51*** (3.551)
Urb $\times$ AUS	-0.81* (0.114)	$Pa/Pm \times$ IRE	-0.93* (0.274)	Urb $\times$ THA	0.64 (0.446)	Land/Labor $\times$ JPN	-1.32*** (0.707)
Urb $\times$ CAN	0.43*** (0.224)	$Pa/Pm \times$ FRA	-0.34** (0.136)	Urb $\times$ IND	-7.84* (1.340)	Urb $\times$ TAI	0.19 (0.167)
Urb $\times$ URU	-0.78* (0.254)	$Pa/Pm \times$ GER	-0.90* (0.247)	Urb $\times$ BUR	-4.10 (2.994)	Urb $\times$ KOR	2.86** (1.111)
Urb $\times$ USA	0.07 (0.101)	$Pa/Pm \times$ SPA	-1.30* (0.407)	Constant	15.29* (2.832)	Urb $\times$ JPN	0.65* (0.178)

Constant	−3.55*	Land/Labor	−0.79*		Constant	−6.26
	(0.713)		(0.097)			(5.500)
		Urbanization	0.41*			
			(0.060)			
		Constant	13.80*			
			(1.376)			
Observations	308		404		226	117
Adjusted R²	0.81		0.69		0.60	0.63

Notes: (*): significant at 1%, (**): significant at 5%, (***) significant at 10%. The first row indicates the coefficient estimates and the second row the standard deviation (in parenthesis). All variables are in natural logarithms, and the estimations are OLS with fixed effects. Urb = urbanization. New World: Argentina (ARG), Australia (AUS), Canada (CAN), Uruguay (URU), and the United States; Europe: Great Britain (GB), Denmark (DEN), France (FRA), Germany (GER), Ireland (IRE), Spain (SPA), and Sweden (SWE); Land-Abundant Asia: Burma (BUR), Egypt (EGY), the Punjab (IND), and Thailand (THA); Land-Scarce Asia: Japan (JPN), Korea (KOR), and Taiwan (TAI).

Source: Williamson (2002b: table 6).

taking hold, and these were primarily in land-scarce parts of the world. With only one exception, table 4.3 confirms this prediction. The coefficient on urbanization is positive and significant for the full sample, for industrial Europe and for industrializing land-scarce East Asia. Furthermore, the coefficient is insignificant for land-abundant Asia, a region where few of the capital-deepening and technologically improving forces of modern economic growth were at work. The exception appears to be the (industrializing) New World, where urbanization is significantly associated with falling, not rising, wage-rental ratios. This exception could, however, be rationalized by an appeal to strong labor-saving technological change there.[12]

The only really disappointing result in table 4.3 is the estimated impact of the endowment ratio. Here we were expecting a positive coefficient, more land per worker raising wages relative to rents. While the expected sign emerges for the New World, it is negative everywhere else. Thus, and contrary to conventional economic intuition, rising land-labor ratios were typically associated with falling, not rising, wage-rental ratios in Europe and Asia. This counter-intuitive result may, of course, reflect omitted variables or reverse causality. First, the omitted variables: land-abundant economies were not often industrial economies, and the latter were becoming more labor scarce, faster. Second, the reverse causality: rather than having exogenous changes in factor endowments drive wage-rental ratios, exogenous changes in commodity prices could have been driving wage-rental ratios, which induced factor supply responses, making land-labor ratios endogenous. The response of the endowment ratio must have been especially elastic in the first global century given the unrestricted north–north migrations within the core and the unrestricted south–south migrations within the periphery. All of these factor supply issues need to be confronted in future research.

Table 4.4 reports what happens when the regressions are modified to reflect regional eccentricities. Things now work better for the New World and land-abundant Asia when we allow the impact of urbanization to be country-specific, for Europe when we allow the impact of Pa/Pm to be country-specific, and for land-scarce East Asia when we allow the impact of endowments to be country-specific. The results reported in table 4.4 are an improvement over those in table 4.3. The wrong sign on the land-labor ratio in East Asia (−0.89, table 4.3) is now shown to be entirely due to Japan's eccentric behavior (JPN, −1.32, table 4.4) since the coefficient on the land-labor ratio in Taiwan (TAI, +2.87) and Korea (KOR, +6.51) is positive, significant, and economically powerful. The magnification effect is also more visible in table 4.4. The negative coefficient on Pa/Pm is now more significant and higher in East Asia (−0.37 versus −0.23); it is still significant and a bit higher in land-abundant Asia (−1.33 versus −1.28) and the New World (−0.67 versus −0.58); and, most strikingly, we now discover it was far above unity in most of Europe—Britain (−1.13), Denmark (−3.94), and Spain (−1.30)—and close to unity in Ireland (−0.93) and Germany (−0.90).

The Connection Between Wage-Rental Ratio and Inequality Trends

Relative factor price convergence had its distribution implications. By inference, labor-scarce regions underwent rising inequality and labor-abundant regions underwent falling inequality. No comprehensive income or wealth distribution data exist to test these assertions for the periphery before 1940, but we do have some useful proxies. Where agriculture looms large in preindustrial economies, where land is the key component of total wealth, and where land ownership is concentrated, the changing wage-rental ratio can indeed be a very effective proxy for inequality trends. Although these lectures do not stress this point, the argument and evidence for it can be found in my previous work (Williamson 1997, 1998, 2000, 2002a) and that in collaboration with Peter Lindert. After all, "changes in the rental-wage ratio tell us how the typical landlord at the top of the distribution did relative to the typical unskilled (landless) worker near the bottom" (Lindert and Williamson 2003: 238), and we have used that fact to motivate the discussion around tables 4.1 and 4.2.

However, we can also appeal to another proxy for inequality trends, the ratio of the unskilled wage to GDP per worker (w/y). Any change in this measure tells us how the unskilled worker near the bottom of the distribution was doing relative to the income recipient in the middle of the distribution. Trends in w/y can be constructed for ten periphery countries 1870–1940 (Argentina, China, India, Indonesia, Japan, Korea, Mexico, Siam, Taiwan, and Uruguay), and they obey almost exactly the same laws of motion as do trends in w/r; w/r and w/y fell together in labor-scarce parts of the periphery, and they rose together in labor-abundant parts of the periphery (Lindert and Williamson 2003: 239–240). For the Atlantic economy, where the evidence is more comprehensive, this correlation extends to trends in actual size distributions of income.

I conclude that trends in w/r and w/y do a good job in capturing trends in income distribution in the periphery between 1870 and 1940.

Absolute Factor Price Divergence versus Relative Factor Price Convergence

I have been talking so far about relative factor prices, not absolute factor prices. I have said nothing about real wages, real incomes, and living standards. While external price shocks can certainly have an impact on real wages and per capita incomes, in the long run they are driven upward almost entirely by technological advance, capital-deepening, and human capital improvement. In most of the poor periphery before 1940, these forces were modest or even absent. After all, this was an epoch during which growth in the core far outstripped that of the periphery, and one during which the gap between the two became so large (Pritchett 1997; Allen 2001a; Bourguignon and Morrisson 2002; Lindert and Williamson 2003).

I stress, however, that there is absolutely nothing inconsistent about the simultaneous appearance of powerful relative factor price convergence and powerful absolute factor price divergence between core and periphery. Globalization forces can explain the relative factor price convergence, as we have seen. But deeper explanations are needed to account for absolute factor price divergence. That is, differences in culture, geography, and institutions will be needed to account for the observed differences in the rates of technical progress and in human capital deepening between core and periphery. Indeed, if technical progress tends to raise the efficiency of all factors, then globalization and commodity price convergence will drive relative factor price convergence with even more certainty. Still, what is striking about pre-1940 world economic experience is that both relative factor price convergence and absolute factor price divergence were so hugely powerful, at the same time.

II

**Impact on Economic
Development and
Policy**

5

The Dark Side: Deindustrialization and Underdevelopment

Deindustrialization in the Periphery

Lecture I concluded that the premodern periphery was integrated into the world economy exactly the way conventional international economics predicts. Spectacular improvements in transport technology worldwide and in factory technology in the industrial core both served to contribute to a trade boom between center and periphery, where the core increasingly specialized in manufactures while the periphery increasingly specialized in primary products. A new international economic order was created (Lewis 1978). In less prosaic terms, the core and the periphery went "to the corners" where their production structures diverged (Krugman and Venables 1995). Alternatively, the core industrialized and the periphery deindustrialized.

Increasing world market integration was manifested by commodity price convergence, and that plus the secular boom in the core served, as we have seen, to improve immensely the terms of trade in the periphery for almost a full century before World War I. The global market integration also served to cause relative factor price convergence worldwide, and the periphery was very much a part of it. In addition, development economists, macroeconomists, and economic historians have shown that the absolute GDP per capita gap between center and periphery also rose hugely over that century. Could one have caused the other? Could globalization-induced deindustrialization in the periphery have helped cause GDP per capita to lag behind there? After all, the positive terms-of-trade shock had its dark side, since it implied a fall in the relative price of manufactures in the periphery, and thus the possibility of deindustrialization.

The idea that the periphery suffered deindustrialization during the first global century has a long pedigree, and while every country has its own independent historiography dealing with the event, the one for India appears to be the longest and the most heated. Both the longevity and the heat may be due partly to the fact that the deindustrialization took place under British rule, partly to the fact that it offers an explanation for persistent Indian poverty until very late in the twentieth century, and partly to the powerful and oft-cited Marxian image of skilled artisans thrown back on the soil. The first official report of Indian deindustrialization seems to have come from Sir William Bentinck, Governor-General of India from 1833 to 1835, whose description of the effect of British mill cloth on the Indian cotton industry was converted into an enduring image by Karl Marx in *Das Kapital*: "The misery hardly finds a parallel in the history of commerce. The bones of the cotton-weavers are bleaching the plains of India" (1977[1867], vol. 1: 558). If that motivation is not sufficient, there are two additional reasons why it might be useful to start by exploring Indian deindustrialization experience before exploring that for the rest of the periphery: Indian deindustrialization accounted for at least a third of total deindustrialization in the periphery; and, surprisingly, it appears that globalization-induced deindustrialization was weaker—the external terms of trade rose less—in India than elsewhere in the periphery.

Measuring Deindustrialization in India 1750–1900

How do we define deindustrialization? David Clingingsmith and I (2004) found a simple 2-good, 3-factor model useful to develop some initial intuition, although it will be expanded later in this chapter. Suppose an economy produces two commodities: agricultural goods, which are exported, and manufactured goods, which are imported. Suppose it uses three factors of production: labor, which is mobile between the two sectors; land, which is used only in agriculture; and capital, which is used only in manufacturing. Suppose further that this economy is what trade economists call a "small country" that takes its terms of trade as exogenous, dictated by world markets. Given these assumptions, deindustrialization can be defined as the movement of labor out of manufacturing and in to agriculture, either measured in absolute numbers (call it weak deindustrialization), or as a share of total employment (call it strong deindustrialization). While de-industrialization is easy enough to define in this simple 2 × 3 framework, an assessment of its short- and long-run impact on living standards and GDP growth is more contentious and hinges on the root causes of deindustrialization.

As defined, the magnitude and timing of deindustrialization in India over the century and a half between 1750 and 1900 is pretty clear. Some time ago, Paul Bairoch (1982) offered evidence to assess de-industrialization not only in India, but across the whole non-European periphery. Table

Table 5.1
World Manufacturing Output 1750–1938 (in percent of total)

Year	India	China	Rest of the Periphery	Developed Core
1750	24.5	32.8	15.7	27.0
1800	19.7	33.3	14.7	32.3
1830	17.6	29.8	13.3	39.5
1880	2.8	12.5	5.6	79.1
1913	1.4	3.6	2.5	92.5
1938	2.4	3.1	1.7	92.8

Source: Simmons (1985), table 1, p. 600, based on Bairoch (1982), tables 10 and 13, pp. 296 and 304.
Note: India refers to the total subcontinent.

5.1 reports his survey as it was retold by Colin Simmons (1985). In 1750, China and India combined to account for almost 57 percent of world manufacturing output, while India itself accounted for almost a quarter. By 1800, India's world share had already eroded to less than a fifth, by 1860 to less than a tenth, and by 1880 to less than 3 percent. Note that India's share in world manufacturing output declined precipitously in the half century 1750–1800, before factory-led industrialization took hold in Britain. Furthermore, per capita manufacturing output fell over the period too (Bairoch 1982: table 4), so it was not just a benign boom in the core at work, but rather a slump in the periphery took place as well. More evidence supporting the magnitude of deindustrialization is offered by the share of manufacturing exports in total exports: between the mid–late-eighteenth century and 1913, that share fell in Asia from about 42 to 21 percent (Findlay and O'Rourke 2003: tables 1.1 and 1.4). Note too that, according to table 5.1, the Indian world manufacturing output share dropped by 4.8 percentage points between 1750 and 1800, when it rose for China and fell by only 1 percentage point for the rest of the periphery. India's share dropped by 6.9 percentage points over the longer period between 1750 and 1830, much bigger than the fall elsewhere (China lost 3 percentage points, and the rest of the periphery lost 2.6 percentage points). Bairoch's data suggest unambiguously that during the century before 1830, well before European factories flooded world markets with manufactures, India suffered much more pronounced deindustrialization than did the rest of the periphery. Perhaps India faced a bigger terms of trade gain than the rest of the periphery. Perhaps geographic endowment had India specializing in the export of primary products that just happened by chance to undergo a bigger relative price rise, in which case it would have undergone a bigger fall in the relative price of manufactures and thus a bigger deindustrialization shock. As we shall see, this was not the case after 1810. Indeed, by comparison India underwent the most modest rise in its terms of trade. Thus, there must have been some exceptional domestic, supply side deindustrialization forces at work in India that complemented the global deindustrialization forces that the whole periphery shared.

Another attempt to measure deindustrialization looks to the early nineteenth century, years that anecdotal evidence has always suggested were ones of most dramatic deindustrialization. Amiya Bagchi (1976a, 1976b) has examined evidence collected between 1809 and 1813 by the East India Company surveyor Buchanan Hamilton on handloom spinning and other traditional industry in Gangetic Bihar, an area of eastern India. Bagchi compared Hamilton's data with the 1901 Census, and the results are presented in table

Table 5.2
Population Dependent on Industry in Gangetic Bihar (in percent of total)

	1809–1813	1901
Assumption A	28.5	8.5
Assumption B	18.6	8.5

Source: Bagchi (1976b): tables 1–5.
Note: Under assumption A, each spinner supports only him or herself, and under assumption B, each spinner also supports one other person. Under both assumptions, nonspinners are assumed to support the survey's modal family size (5).

5.2 using two alternative assumptions. The table suggests a substantial decline in the industrial employment share during the nineteenth century, ranging from 10 to 20 percentage points.

While the employment share in "other industrial" occupations fell over the century as well, table 5.3 makes it clear that a very large share of this deindustrialization had its source in the decline of cotton spinning.[1] Since cotton spinning was performed at home using extremely simple technology, it may seem implausible to argue that the demise of cotton spinning in the early nineteenth century destroyed India's platform for modern industrialization. Yet British economic historians assign the same importance to home-based cotton spinning: seventeenth- and eighteenth-century "protoindustrial" putting-out systems and cottage industries are said to have supplied the platform for the factory-based British industrial revolution that followed (Mokyr 1993: chapters 1–3), and employment of women and children was central to the process then too (De Vries 1994). Indeed, they coexisted with the factories for some time: "until the 1830s . . . decentralized, workshop, artisan and putting-out systems were successful and profitable, and . . .

Table 5.3
Percentage of Total Population of Gangetic Bihar Dependent on Different
Occupations (in percent of total)

	1809–1813	1901
Spinners	10.3	} 1.3
Weavers	2.4	
Other industrial	9.0	7.2
TOTAL	21.6*	8.5

Source: Bagchi (1976b): tables 1–5.
* Bagchi reports a total of 18.6, but this appears to be an error, apart from
rounding.

compatible with a substantial degree of technological
change" (Berg 1994: 133–134).

Subcontracting and putting-out to family workers at
home was common in Britain until well into the nineteenth
century, and "smaller- and medium-scale manufactures
held the stage for most of the industrial revolution" (Berg
1994: 144).

Finally, in an unpublished study reported by Irfan Habib
(1985), Amalendu Guha documented a huge decline in yarn
used for Indian handloom production, from 419 million
pounds in 1850, to 240 in 1870, and to 221 in 1900. This indi-
rect evidence suggests that the decline in hand spinning
documented for Gangetic Bihar in the early nineteenth
century was widespread, that it was followed by a decline
in hand weaving during the midcentury, and that the
decline of both hand spinning and weaving was almost
complete by 1870. This latter point is also confirmed by
Bairoch's per capita manufacturing output figures (1982:
table 4): somewhere between 1860 and 1928, the index
bottoms out and starts to rise for both China and India,
while it soars after 1860 for Japan.

Debating the Causes of Indian Deindustrialization

What were the likely causes of the deindustrialization? Of course the answer will be influenced by the magnitude of the terms of trade shock, and that will depend on the commodities exported (Diaz-Alejandro 1984). In addition, I think we will only get the right answer if we distinguish between domestic- and foreign-induced forces, and if we also distinguish between tradables and nontradables.

The first and most popular possible cause lies with those world-market-induced price shocks that served to lower the relative price of manufactures worldwide. Those countries exporting manufactures and importing primary products underwent unfavorable terms of trade trends since they had to share their rapid productivity gains in manufacturing with the rest of the world by absorbing a fall in their export prices. Those countries exporting primary products and importing manufactures enjoyed favorable terms-of-trade trends that clearly raised their GDP in the short run. But those trends also penalized import-competing manufacturing in the periphery. Thus, whether a secular rise in its terms of trade also raised periphery GDP in the long run depended on its deindustrialization impact. If industrialization is a carrier of growth—as most growth theories imply,[2] then deindustrialization could lead to a growth slowdown and a low-income equilibrium that gives deindustrialization its power in the historical literature.

The second possible cause of periphery deindustrialization might have been a strengthening in the primary-product export sector's comparative advantage, either due to productivity advance there or increasing accessibility of its exports to the world economy. In the first case, and still retaining the small country assumption, nothing would have happened to the terms of trade. In the second case, the country would have enjoyed an unambiguous terms of trade improvement as declining world trade barriers raised export prices and lowered import prices in the home market. Whether living standards of landless labor also increased would have depended on the direction of the terms-of-trade change and whether the primary product was food, and, if so, whether it dominated the worker's budget. Most importantly, and once again, deindustrialization could have led to a growth slowdown and a low-income equilibrium.

The third possible cause of periphery deindustrialization might have been a deterioration at home in manufacturing productivity and competitiveness. In this case, and still retaining the small country assumption, nothing would have happened to the terms of trade, but real wages and living standards would have deteriorated, and so would have GDP. The economic impact of deindustrialization from this source is unambiguous. But why the deterioration in manufacturing competitiveness at home? In the Indian case, could it have been due to the decline in agricultural productivity, perhaps due in part to a collapse in Mughal authority, a once-powerful empire that reached a low ebb in the middle of the eighteenth century?

If some of the observed deindustrialization was due to the demise of the Mughal Empire, exactly how did it work? To see the mechanism I have in mind more clearly, the simple 2×3 Heckscher-Ohlin model needs to be converted into a more realistic 3×4 Ricardian model that adds a (big) non-tradable grain sector[3] and makes land specific to grains or commodity exportables so that arable cannot be switched between them. Now, to the extent that the decline of the Mughals had an asymmetric negative impact on productivity in agriculture, the price of the key nontradable (grain) relative to the key importable (textiles) would have increased. Since grain (mainly rice and wheat) was the dominant consumption good for workers, and if the grain wage was close to subsistence, this negative productivity shock should have put upward pressure on the nominal wage in cotton hand spinning and weaving, wages that started from a low nominal but high real base in the early eighteenth century (Parthasarathi 1998; Allen 2001b). If this rise in the "own" wage in textiles was big enough, it should have taken away the competitive edge India had in booming third-country export markets (e.g., "cheap labor").

Perhaps this is the reason why eighteenth-century Britain was able to wrest away India's long-standing leadership in the fastest-growing world markets—West Africa and the Americas, where cheap calicos were clothing the booming slave labor force, and Europe. English merchants and English ships were the main suppliers to the Atlantic trade, a lot of it involved the (Indian) re-export trade.[4] The share of West African trade claimed by Indian textiles was about 38 percent in the 1730s, 22 percent in the 1780s, and 3 percent in the 1840s (Inikori 2002: 512–513, 516). By the end of the seventeenth century, Indian calicos were a major force in European markets (Landes 1998: 154). For example, the share of total English trade with southern Europe claimed by Indian textiles was more than 20 percent in the 1720s, but this share fell to about 6 percent in the 1780s and less than 4 percent in the 1840s (Inikori 2002: 517). India was already losing its world market share in textiles during the eighteenth century, long before the industrial revolution took hold firmly in Britain.[5]

Which explanation works best in accounting for India's deindustrialization? I see Indian deindustrialization as

evolving through three distinct epochs over the two centuries following 1750, each driven by quite different forces.
The second is much better understood than the first and
third.

The first epoch, approximately 1750–1810, was one during
which India lost its significant share of world textile markets
to Britain. What was an important export sector in India
at the beginning of the epoch became an important
import-competing sector at the end. While the switch can
be explained by increasing cost competitiveness favoring
Britain, superior factory technology was not yet the main
force at work. Instead, it appears that the demise of the
Mughal Empire mattered most in this epoch, a force that
lowered agricultural productivity in India, raised grain
prices there, and thus—in a relatively stable real wage subsistence economy where grain was the key consumption
good—pushed up nominal wages economy-wide. Hence,
the own-wage rose in the import-competing manufacturing
sector and in the primary-product export sector,[6] damaging
cost competitiveness in both.

It should be added that I am hardly the first to exploit
the connection between labor productivity in preindustrial
agriculture, nominal wages in manufacturing, and the
resulting competitiveness in world markets for manufactures. Alexander Gerschenkron (1962) and W. Arthur Lewis
(1978: chapter 2) have both used the argument to good effect
in explaining why low productivity in agriculture helps
explain the absence or delay of industrial revolutions. More
recently, and as I suggested above, Parthasarathi (1998) has
argued that while high farm productivity produced living
standards in the south of India that were just as high as that
in the south of England, that high productivity also produced low grain prices. Low grain prices made possible the

low nominal wages that gave India a ("cheap labor") edge in world textile markets. A generation before Parthasarathi, Tapan Raychaudhuri set forth a similar view of Mughal India (Raychaudhuri 1983: 5–6, 16–18, 32).

The second epoch, approximately 1810–1860, is the classic deindustrialization episode when India lost so much of its domestic textile market to Britain. This loss can be explained by the combined influence of relatively rapid factory-based productivity advance in Britain and by increased world market integration, the latter driven by declining transport costs between the two trading partners, and to a free trade commitment (although as the colony, India had little choice in the matter). The terms of trade moved to favor India and thus penalized import-competing manufacturing there. The effects of the demise of the Mughal Empire were only a memory, and the induced decline in Indian grain productivity had ceased.

The third epoch, following 1860, was one during which the rate of deindustrialization slowed down and eventually turned around to become "reindustrialization." This result can be explained by the subsidence in both the unbalanced productivity advance favoring European manufacturing and in the world transport revolution. The terms of trade no longer moved in India's favor and thus no longer served to penalize import competing manufacturing. Indeed, to the extent that the terms of trade started its long-run downward slide after the 1860s or 1880s, import-competing manufacturing should have received a stimulus in India and in the rest of the periphery.

The Relative Price Evidence from India

Are these predictions confirmed by the relative price and real wage evidence? It appears that they are.

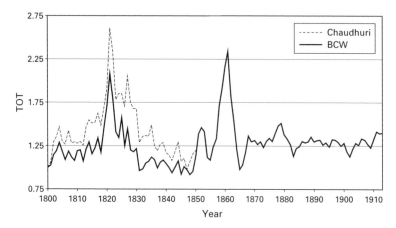

Figure 5.1
Terms of trade for India 1800–1913
Source: Clingingsmith and Williamson (2004: figure 6).

Let us begin with the external terms of trade. Figure 5.1 is only able to document the terms of trade starting in 1800, but it shows two big spurts in the second epoch, the first over the decade of the 1810s and the second over the decade of the 1850s. If there was any trend in the terms of trade over the half century that favored India (and thus penalized the import competing sector), it was very modest. But Px/Pm trends only measure the relative price changes between the two tradable sectors. To the extent that it was dictated in world markets, these relative price trends would have given an incentive for resources to migrate from the import-competing sector to the export sector. What about the tradable sectors relative to the big nontradable sector, grains? Did those relative prices behave in a way such as to pull labor out of grain production and in to textiles or in to primary-product exports? No. Figure 5.2 shows that, relative to grains, the price of primary-product exportables (Pc)

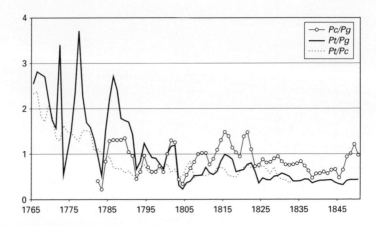

Figure 5.2
Relative prices of tradeables (1800 = 1)
Source: A revision of Clingingsmith and Williamson (2004: figure 2).

and textile importables (*Pt*) fell after 1810 and especially
after 1815. If Indian textiles were a technologically dynamic
sector, then the fall in *Pt/Pg* would not have been so damaging. But it was not: all of the fall in *Pt* was being driven
by dynamic technological events outside India.

Now let us consider relative price behavior across the first
two epochs combined (also figure 5.2). Between 1765 and
1810, the price of textiles relative to grains fell at a spectacular rate: by 1805–1810, it was less than a fifth of its
1765–1770 level. The decline continued after 1810, but at a
much slower rate. Why the spectacular fall in *Pt/Pg* in the
late eighteenth century, especially compared with the early
nineteenth century? The answer is that grain prices soared
upwards in the long run. Did this reduce real wages (*w/Pg*)?
Apparently not: the grain wage fell only very modestly
between the late 1760s and the 1810s (figure 5.3). True, there
was great short-run volatility in the grain wage, but a Lewis-

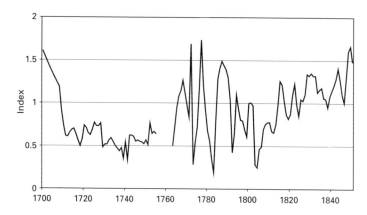

Figure 5.3
Grain wage in India 1700–1850 (1800 = 1)
Source: Clingingsmith and Williamson (2004: figure 3).

like assumption (Lewis 1954) about long-run, real-wage stability seems to be roughly confirmed for the first epoch. Note, however, that the own-wage in Indian manufacturing more than doubled between 1765 and 1810 (figure 5.4: w/Pt)! Since there is no qualitative evidence suggesting significant productivity advance in Indian textiles or in other manufacturing activities during this epoch, I take this as powerful support for the thesis that the demise of the Mughal Empire, the resulting collapse in agricultural productivity, the induced rise in (nontradable) grain prices, and the subsequent escalation of nominal wages economy-wide can indeed explain much of the erosion in India's competitiveness in its textile industry, its loss of world markets, and thus its deindustrialization.

Grain prices stopped their secular rise after around 1810, and the upward pressure on nominal wages must therefore have eased. The damage to agricultural productivity had

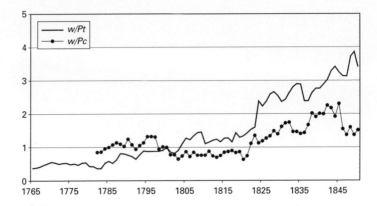

Figure 5.4
Indian own wages in textiles and agricultural export commodities (1800 = 1)
Source: Clingingsmith and Williamson (2004: figure 4).

been done, British authority had begun to fill the void left
by the collapse of the Mughal authority, and conditions in
the grain sector stabilized. Thus, it would appear that the
fall in *Pt*—induced by productivity events abroad that were
not reproduced at home—now dominated deindustrialization conditions in Indian manufacturing. The relative price
Pt/Pg fell (figure 5.2), the own-wage *w/Pt* rose (figure 5.4),
and deindustrialization continued—but all three were now
driven mainly by world market forces. This interpretation is
consistent with the conventional deindustrialization narrative, but by failing to make an explicit comparison between
England and India, it misses the supporting role of relatively
poor productivity growth in Indian grain cultivation.

  If we take the own-wage in manufacturing as a critical
indicator of cost competitiveness, and if England was
India's main competitor in world markets, it seems relevant
to compare trends in textiles' own-wage between the two.
Our source for England is Gregory Clark (2004), whose data

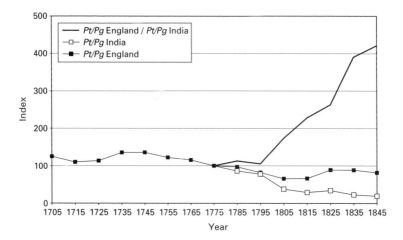

Figure 5.5
Grain price of textiles in England and India (1775 = 100)
Source: Clingingsmith and Williamson (2004: figure 5a).

allow the construction of the price of clothing relative to grain (Pt/Pg) 1705–1865 and the own-wage in textiles (w/Pt). Figure 5.5 plots an index of the ratio of English to Indian Pt/Pg. The price of textiles relative to grains fell in both economies 1765–1850, but it fell five times faster in India. Pt/Pg fell much slower in England than India (due to the much bigger Pg boom in India) so that the index rose to 228 by 1815 (1775 = 100), and to 421 by 1845. Grain prices rose almost four times faster in India than England, an event that put greater upward pressure on wage costs in India than England, thus lowering the English own-wage in textiles relative to India. Indeed, the ratio of w/Pt in England relative to India fell from 100 in 1775, to 56 in 1815, and to 26 in 1845, as shown in figure 5.6. Sixty percent of that secular fall over the seven decades 1775–1845 was completed after three decades, before the great flood of factory-produced textiles

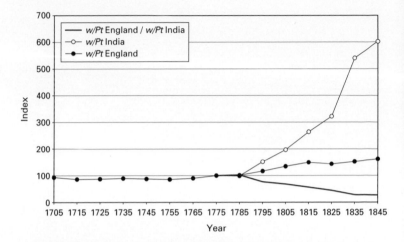

Figure 5.6
Textile own wages in England and India (1775 = 100)
Source: Clingingsmith and Williamson (2004: figure 5b).

hit Indian markets in the second epoch of deindustrialization.[7] To the extent that textile prices were closely linked between England and India, the much bigger rise in relative grain prices in India must have had a great deal to do with rapid farm productivity advance in England compared with its stagnancy in India.

This evidence seems to point to the decline of the Mughal Empire and agricultural productivity as the central cause of Indian deindustrialization in the eighteenth century. It also looks like poor productivity performance in Indian agriculture even helps explain deindustrialization during the first half of the nineteenth century when those globalization forces were doing their better known work. This conclusion is consistent with the fact that deindustrialization during the first half of the century was far more dramatic in India than in the rest of the periphery, even though the external terms of trade shock was a lot smaller.

What about the Rest of the Periphery?

Deindustrialization appeared everywhere around the nineteenth-century periphery, and globalization plays a major role in each region's economic history narrative. However, these regional economic histories rarely make comparative quantitative assessments,[8] thus ignoring one way to decompose the sources of periphery deindustrialization into internal supply side and external global forces. Here I only ask whether nineteenth-century India faced a big or a small deindustrializing global price shock compared with other parts of the periphery. If it was relatively small, then the domestic deindustrialization forces I have documented here must have been more important in India than they were elsewhere in the periphery.

If we ignore the few years around 1820 when the terms of trade spikes, it appears that India underwent relatively modest improvements in its terms of trade from 1800 to the mid-1820s, and in fact it fell thereafter up to 1850 (figure 5.1). Over the half century between 1800–1804 and 1855–1859, India's terms of trade rose "only" 28.6 percent, or less than 0.5 percent per annum. No doubt this was a significant secular price shock, but it was far smaller than what happened in other parts of the periphery. The Latin American terms of trade increased by 1.7 percent per annum between 1820–1824 and 1855–1859 (figure 5.8: Bértola and Williamson 2005: figure 2), more than three times that of India. The Ottoman terms of trade increased by 2.4 percent per annum between 1815–1819 and 1855–1859 (figure 5.7: Williamson database) while the Indonesian terms of trade

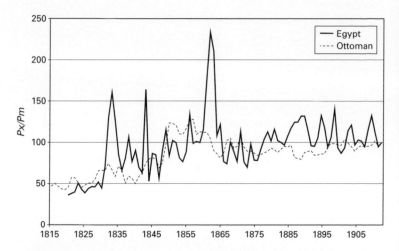

Figure 5.7
Terms of trade for Egypt and the Ottoman Empire 1815–1913 (1913 = 100)

increased by 2.5 percent per annum between 1825–1829 and
1865–1869 (figure 5.8: Korthals Altes 1994: 159–160), both
almost five times that of India. The Egyptian terms of trade
rose by 2.7 percent per annum between 1820–1824 and
1855–1859 (figure 5.7: Williamson database), more than
five times that of India. East Asia offers the most dramatic
comparison: recall from above that over the fifteen years
following Japan's emergence from isolation in 1858, its
terms of trade rose by a factor of 3.5 or 4.9!

External price shocks facing India were, therefore, quite
modest compared to the rest of the periphery, or even compared with the rest of Asia. Yet, Indian historians complain
the most about deindustrialization. It seems to me that
domestic supply-side conditions must have played a far
more important role in accounting for deindustrialization in
India than elsewhere. Furthermore, it can hardly be a coin-
cidence that "reindustrialization" started in much of the

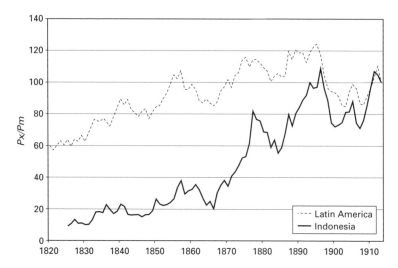

Figure 5.8
Terms of trade for Latin America and Indonesia 1820–1913 (1913 = 100)

periphery after the 1860s when the secular rise in its terms of trade slowed down and then fell. The terms-of-trade boom lasted longer in Latin America, where it continued to rise up to the late 1880s. It is said that Latin America exploited the global boom following midcentury better than the rest of the periphery (Bulmer-Thomas 1994), and its comparative terms-of-trade experience offers a reason why. Furthermore, there is also absolutely no evidence of a booming manufacturing sector in late nineteenth-century Latin America while there is plenty of such evidence for the Bombay Presidency, the greater Shanghai region, Japan, and the European periphery. While different supply-side conditions at home mattered, comparative terms of trade experience offers an additional explanation for these regional differences around the periphery.

For regions in the periphery exporting primary products, a secular improvement in the terms of trade penalized the import-competing sector and suppressed industrialization, while a secular deterioration did the opposite. While domestic supply-side forces also mattered, globalization and rapid manufacturing productivity advance in the core clearly contributed to deindustrialization in the periphery during most of the century before World War I. In the words of W. Arthur Lewis (1978: 67–75), were these global forces an engine of growth in the periphery? Or, instead, was the impact of globalization-induced deindustrialization so powerful that it suppressed GDP growth there?

6

Terms-of-Trade Impact: Secular Trend and Volatility

Prebisch, Singer, and the Secular Terms-of-Trade Deterioration Debate

Debate over trends in the terms of trade between primary products and manufactures, their causes, and their impact has dominated the trade and development literature for more than a century. Classical economists claimed that the relative price of primary commodities should improve over time, since land and other natural resources are in inelastic supply while capital and labor are not. As we have seen, the experience over the century before 1860 proved them right: the relative price of manufactures underwent a spectacular decline, while that of primary products soared. In the early 1950s, however, Hans Singer and Raúl Prebisch challenged the classical view, asserting that the terms of trade of the primary-product–producing Third World had deteriorated since the late-nineteenth century.[1] They also projected that it would continue to deteriorate across the late-twentieth century as long as the Third World specialized in primary products. While faster technological progress in manufactures may have caused the price of primary products to rise relative to manufactures over most of the nineteenth century, Prebisch and Singer also noted that this secular trend had reversed. Indeed, Prebisch calculated that only 63 percent of the finished manufactures that could be bought with a given quantity of primary products in the 1860s could be purchased in the 1930s. These secular trends also implied a long-run stimulus to import-competing industry in the periphery, but Prebisch worried more about the short-run economic damage since the periphery was so committed to primary-product exports. Indeed, in 1890–1909 Latin America devoted 97 percent of its exports to primary products, Asia and the Middle East 90 percent, while the European industrial core devoted only 30 percent of their total exports to such products (table 6.1, column 6). A new economic order was in place, with the poor periphery exporting primary products in exchange for manufactures.

In lecture I, we saw that the terms of trade for a small sample of primary-product–exporting regions rose between the 1870s and World War I, a secular rise that had started a half century before. On average, it rose by much less between the 1890s and World War I, and it even fell in some parts of the periphery. But it fell everywhere in the periphery afterwards, and that the subsequent fall to the 1930s erased any secular post-1870 gains, consistent with the Prebisch calculation. This secular decline in the terms of trade of primary products between the 1870s and the 1930s is confirmed again with the larger sample underlying figures 6.1 and 6.2: for Asia, the fall from its 1870s peak to its 1930s trough was 29 percent; for Latin America, the fall from its 1885–1895 peak to its 1930s trough was 40 percent. This secular decline was used to support the move towards Third World autarky in the 1940s, 1950s, and 1960s, a highly interventionist industrialization strategy that eventually came to

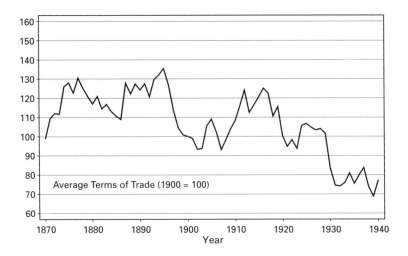

Figure 6.1
Terms of trade for Latin America 1870–1940
Source: Blattman, Hwang, and Williamson (2004: figure 4c).

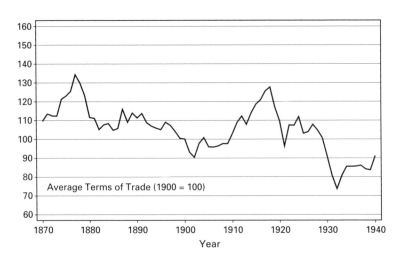

Figure 6.2
Terms of trade for Asia and the Middle East 1870–1940
Source: Clingingsmith and Williamson (2004: figure 4d).

Table 6.1
Profile of the Core and Periphery

	1870–1889			
	GDP per Capita	Primary Products as a Percent of Exports	Top 2 Exports as a Percent of Top 5 Exports	Exports as a Percent of GDP
PERIPHERY				
European "Frontier" Offshoots				
Australia	4,442	97	98	15
Canada	1,822	95	96	12
New Zealand	3,668	99	100	16
	3,311	97	98	15
Latin America				
Argentina	1,676	100	87	15
Brazil	755	100	86	17
Chile	1,185	99	100	22
Colombia	1,113	99	100	4
Cuba	1,647	80	[a]	49
Mexico	835	100	99	4
Peru	497	99	74	24
Uruguay	1,676	100	74	22
	1,173	97	89	20
Asia and the Middle East				
Burma (Myanmar)	628	91	100	14
Ceylon (Sri Lanka)	730	98	100	11
China	565	98	73	1
Egypt	369	93	100	29
India	660	98	55	4
Indonesia	581	91	—	3
Japan	800	71	100	1
Philippines	955	96	81	5

	1890–1909				1920–1939		
GDP per Capita	Primary Products as a Percent of Exports	Top 2 Exports as a Percent of Top 5 Exports	Exports as a Percent of GDP	GDP per Capita	Primary Products as Percent of Exports	Top 2 Exports as a Percent of Top 5 Exports	Exports as a Percent of GDP
4,394	97	84	20	5,268	96	76	15
2,801	91	68	15	3,993	74	51	19
4,295	96	89	23	5,232	99	69	25
3,830	95	81	19	4,831	89	65	20
2,823	99	58	19	3,912	99	47	14
749	100	91	21	1,087	100	92	9
1,923	99	100	19	2,800	100	100	12
1,034	99	100	6	1,486	99	100	7
1,825	83	100	41	1,440	96	100	41
1,183	100	86	5	1,463	99	62	7
802	99	55	10	1,451	100	67	12
2,823	100	72	19	3,912	100	85	18
1,645	97	83	17	2,194	99	82	15
622	86	93	12	751	98	83	45
932	98	100	13	1,114	98	100	15
648	93	66	1	769	85	43	1
487	96	100	25	650	97	100	18
723	96	51	5	1,083	97	59	6
629	86	60	4	651	75	54	4
1,108	70	99	4	1,948	44	89	7
1,086	95	90	4	1,527	91	81	5

Table 6.1

(continued)

	1870–1889			
	GDP per Capita	Primary Products as a Percent of Exports	Top 2 Exports as a Percent of Top 5 Exports	Exports as a Percent of GDP
Siam (Thailand)	751	99	100	2
Turkey	831	99	50	6
	834	92	83	4
European Periphery				
Greece	1,343	94	[a]	7
Portugal	1,151	96	75	6
Russia/USSR	976	97	79	4
Serbia/Yugoslavia	852	96	73	6
Spain	1,588	73	64	5
	1,182	91	73	5
CORE				
Industrial Leaders				
France	2,119	43	[b]	13
Germany	2,184	38	[b]	9
United Kingdom	3,598	12	[b]	14
United States	2,952	86	[b]	6
	2,713	45	—	10
European Industrial Latecomers				
Austria/Austria-Hungary	1,108	35	[b]	9
Denmark	2,105	96	[a]	14
Italy	1,516	87	[b]	6
Norway	1,446	90	100	13
Sweden	1,875	85	[b]	9
	1,610	79	—	10

Sources: Blattman, Hwang, and Williamson (2004), table 1.
Notes: a. No data available for this period. b. Data for the Industrial Leaders and most European Latecomers not available in standard secondary sources.

	1890–1909				1920–1939		
GDP per Capita	Primary Products as a Percent of Exports	Top 2 Exports as a Percent of Top 5 Exports	Exports as a Percent of GDP	GDP per Capita	Primary Products as Percent of Exports	Top 2 Exports as a Percent of Top 5 Exports	Exports as a Percent of GDP
811	99	100	6	815	98	87	7
941	97	59	9	936	92	72	5
987	90	87	6	1,307	81	82	6
,487	90	73	7	2,321	96	86	4
,348	92	73	7	1,562	75	85	7
,178	96	73	4	1,593	85	48	1
944	96	77	7	1,225	92	64	5
2,009	75	46	7	2,557	80	[a]	4
,393	90	69	6	1,852	86	71	4
2,739	40	[b]	15	4,100	35	[b]	10
3,007	33	[b]	9	4,001	24	[b]	11
,419	17	[b]	14	5,112	22	[b]	12
,126	80	[b]	6	5,969	57	[b]	5
,573	43	—	11	4,795	35	—	9
,545	41	[b]	9	3,211	35	[b]	10
2,913	96	88	22	4,791	90	91	20
,784	74	[b]	7	2,888	48	[b]	5
,763	74	94	18	3,126	64	100	20
2,483	75	[b]	12	3,722	58	[b]	15
2,098	72	—	13	3,548	59	—	14

be called import substitution industrialization (ISI). While Hans Singer also advocated this antiglobal ISI strategy, he noted that if the post-1950 relative price of primary-products ever did improve, it would reduce industrialization incentives in the periphery (Singer 1950: 482). Thus, while a post-1950 improvement in the primary-product exporter's terms of trade might augment incomes in the short run, a good thing, Singer thought it was also likely to suppress industrialization in the long run, a bad thing. No one seemed to pay much attention to Singer's aside at that time, including Singer himself.

Many modern economists have reached Singer's conclusion, but for different reasons. Some have argued that resources are a "curse" to development, such that while an improvement in the terms of trade facing primary-product exporters would increase the value of the resource base being exploited, poor growth would result. Jeffrey Sachs and Andrew Warner (2001) have confirmed the correlation, but economists have not yet agreed on how the "resource curse" works. Some argue that resource-abundant poor countries have undeveloped property rights such that terms-of-trade booms get translated into capital flight (a transfer of rents for safe keeping in rich countries: Tornell and Velasco 1992). Others make the case for growth-suppressing rent-seeking (Krueger 1974; Murphy, Shleifer, and Vishny 1993; Baland and Francois 2000) and to growth-distorting government policy (Tornell and Lane 1999). Still others favor crowding-out and Dutch disease, a position these lectures also favor. Initiated first by Max Corden (1981, 1984) and Corden and Peter Neary (1982), a huge literature has developed over the past twenty-five years that has examined how manufacturing in modern economies has been affected by the discovery of tradable natural resources or by an increase in their price. The name "Dutch disease" is taken from the impact of natural gas price increases on the Dutch economy in the 1970s. The most extensive applications, however, have been to Third World economies that specialize in primary products. There have been far fewer applications of deindustrialization and Dutch disease models to the development in the periphery over the 150 or so years before the modern late-twentieth century experience. Whichever view one supports, the Sachs-Warner correlation has also been found in the more distant past: my earlier work with Yael Hadass (Hadass and Williamson 2003) found that for a small sample of primary-product exporters between 1870 and World War I poor growth did ensue following the terms-of-trade improvement, lending some limited support to resource curse theories.

Others have argued for the more benign classical view where an increase in the price of the primary product export raises the expected rate of return on investment in that sector, thus augmenting accumulation and growth economy-wide. Using a cross-country panel of forty countries from 1970 to 1991, Enrique Mendoza (1997) did indeed find that an increase in the growth rate of the terms of trade by 1 percent raised the growth rate of consumption by 0.2 percent, although most of the developing countries in his sample were exporting labor-intensive manufactures by the end of the period.[2] Still, Michael Bleaney and David Greenway (2001) used Mendoza's model to analyze sub-Saharan Africa between 1980 and 1995, where primary product exports still dominated (at least up to the early 1990s[3]), finding that both GDP per capita growth and investment increased as the terms of trade improved.

The Prebisch-Singer primary-product terms-of-trade deterioration thesis has not survived the half century since they wrote, since we now think that structural breaks, serially correlated residuals, and unit roots may explain the twentieth-century patterns we see. Thus, Enzo Grilli and Maw Cheng Yang (1988) analyzed twentieth-century commodity price data and found evidence of periodic structural breaks, but no trend. Bleaney and Greenway (1993) contested this finding, but were able to document only a modest downward trend. Furthermore, and to repeat, most of the periphery was little damaged by this modest secular deterioration since by the 1990s the majority had shifted out of primary-product exports and into labor-intensive manufacture exports. Thus, from today's vantage point, the Prebisch-Singer secular deterioration hypothesis, and its implied negative impact, can be rejected. It is not clear, however, that it should be rejected from the vantage point of 1950 when Singer and Prebisch were looking backward to the 1870s. Nor has the modern literature yet told us what the impact of the terms-of-trade deterioration had on long-run GDP per capita growth in the periphery.

The jury is still out. What we need is a larger sample of periphery countries, and we need it for the period that motivated the Prebisch-Singer debate in the first place. It will prove difficult to construct the necessary database for the pre-1870 century, but we can do it for the post-1870 century. When the terms of trade of primary products deteriorated between the 1860s and the 1940s, what was its economic impact on the periphery? The answer hinges on two additional questions: When and where in the periphery did the terms of trade deteriorate? When it did deteriorate, and thus when the relative price of import competing manufactures rose, was long run GDP growth stimulated by induced industrialization enough to overcome the short-run losses from the terms-of-trade fall?

Terms-of-Trade Volatility and Economic Growth

Until the last three decades or so, most countries in the periphery specialized in the export of just a handful of commodities (table 6.1, columns 3, 7, and 11). In the 1920s, for example, the top two exports were 82 percent of all exports from the average Third World country. Furthermore, some of these commodities were more volatile than others, and those countries with more volatile primary-product prices have grown slowly relative to the industrial leaders and to other primary-product exporters. Figure 6.3 charts income per head in 1939 against volatility in the terms of trade for 35 countries between 1870 and 1939.[4] Volatility is measured as the standard deviation of departures from a slow-moving trend.[5] The figure clearly depicts a negative correlation

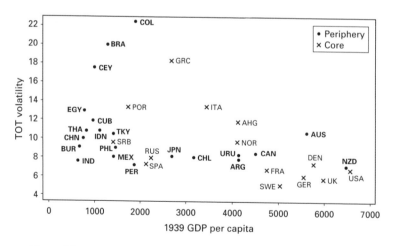

Figure 6.3
1939 GDP per capita and terms-of-trade volatility 1870–1939
Source: Blattman, Hwang, and Williamson (2004), Figure 1.

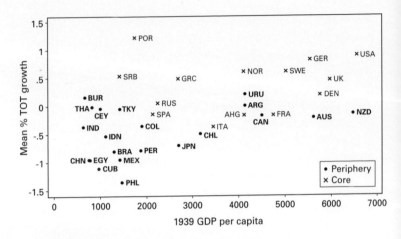

Figure 6.4
1939 GDP per capita and mean terms-of-trade growth 1870–1939
Source: Blattman, Hwang, and Williamson (2004: figure 2).

between terms-of-trade volatility and subsequent level of development, not just in the total sample but also within the subset of primary product-specialized countries in the periphery. Figure 6.4 charts 1939 income per head against the secular trend in the terms of trade. Within both the periphery and the core, we see a positive correlation between growth in the terms of trade and subsequent level of development. As noted before, these correlations are reminiscent of what Carlos Diaz-Alejandro (1984) called the commodity lottery. He argued that each country's exportable resources were determined in large part by geography (plus the previous century's experience with global market integration), and that differences in subsequent economic development were a consequence of the economic, political, and institutional attributes of each commodity.

So far, this lecture has focused on secular terms of trade movements and their implications for industrialization and deindustrialization, but could it be that exogenous price volatility of each primary product also mattered by generating internal instability, reduced investment, and diminished economic growth? Observers regularly point to terms-of-trade shocks as a key source of macroeconomic instability in commodity-specialized countries, but they pay far less attention to the long-run growth implications of such instabilty.[6] Most theories stress the investment channel in looking for connections between terms-of-trade instability and growth. Indeed, the development literature offers an abundance of microeconomic evidence linking income volatility to lower investment in both physical and human capital. Households imperfectly protected from risk change their income-generating activities in the face of income volatility, diversifying toward low-risk alternatives with lower average returns (Dercon 2004; Fafchamps 2004), as well as to lower levels of investment (Rosenweig and Wolpin 1993). Furthermore, severe cuts in health and education seem to follow negative shocks to household income in poor countries—cuts that disproportionately affect children and hence long-term human capital accumulation (Jacoby and Skoufias 1997; Frankenburg, Beegle, Sikoki, and Thomas 1999; Jensen 2000; Thomas et al. 2004).

Poor households and poor firms find it difficult to smooth their consumption and investment in the face of shocks because they are rationed in credit and insurance markets. Poor governments also find it difficult to borrow internationally, especially at cheap rates, making it hard to smooth public investment and expenditure in the face of terms-of-trade shocks.[7] Garey and Valerie Ramey (1995) examined the macroeconomic volatility and growth correlation using data from ninety-two developing and developed economies between 1962 and 1985. They found government spending and macroeconomic volatility to be inversely related, and that countries with higher volatility had lower mean growth. Domestic and foreign investment should respond to such volatility. Likewise, higher volatility in the terms of trade should reduce investment and growth in the presence of risk aversion. What is true of the modern era was probably even more true of the premodern era when undeveloped financial institutions and a limited tax base made it even harder for poor households, poor firms, and poor governments to smooth expenditures.

The Jury Is In: The Impact of Secular Trend and Volatility in Periphery Terms of Trade 1870–1939

There are thirty-five countries in the historical sample[8] that Chris Blattman, Jason Hwang, and I used recently (Blattman, Hwang and Williamson 2004) to explore these issues: fourteen in the core and twenty-one in the periphery, although the results are robust to every plausible core-periphery allocation explored. Table 6.1 lists the thirty-five by GDP per capita, the dominance of primary products in exports, export concentration, and export shares in GDP. The impact of secular change and volatility in the terms of trade are presented in table 6.2. Results are displayed for the full seven decades (1870–1939) as well as for two subperiods, the first global century from 1870 to 1909 and the interwar autarkic disaster from 1920 to 1939.[9] The World War I decade is omitted throughout.

The results are reported separately for the core and periphery, making it possible to test for the presence of asymmetry between them. Asymmetry is predicted by the following reasoning. Consider secular impact first. To the extent that the periphery specializes in primary products, and to the extent that industry is a carrier of development, then positive price shocks reinforce specialization in the periphery and cause deindustrialization there, offsetting the short-run gains from the terms-of-trade improvement. There is no offset in the core, but rather there is a strengthening, since specialization in industrial products is reinforced there by an improvement in the terms of trade. Thus, the prediction is that while a terms-of-trade improvement unambiguously raises growth rates in the industrial core, it does not in the periphery. I expect the same asymmetry with respect to terms-of-trade volatility to the extent that "insurance" is cheaper and more widely available in the core. For example, to the extent that core governments have a much wider range of tax sources, their tax revenues should be more stable in response to terms-of-trade shocks than should be true of periphery governments that rely instead on tariffs and export taxes. The induced macroinstability should have suppressed accumulation in risk-adverse periphery countries: poor governments should have invested less in their infrastructure; poor parents should have invested less in the education of themselves and their children; and poor firms should have invested less in new products and new technologies.

Table 6.2 also reports results with and without a term interacting terms-of-trade growth (TOT Trend Growth) with export share of GDP to see whether the terms-of-trade impact was contingent upon the level of export dependence. It seems reasonable that more export-oriented countries would respond more forcefully to external shocks. Export shares are taken from the first year of the decade to avoid problems of endogeneity.

Table 6.2
GDP Growth and the Terms of Trade, 1870–1939

Dependent Variable: Decadal Average GDP per capita growth
TOT Growth Measure: Decadal growth in a Hodrick-Prescott filtered trend
TOT Volatility Measure: Decadal standard deviation of annual departures from trend

	(1)	(2)	(3)	(4)
	1870–1939 (1910–1919 excluded)			
	Core	Periphery	Core	Periphery
TOT trend growth	0.411 [0.181]**	–0.041 [0.135]	0.735 [0.319]**	–0.378 [0.153]**
TOT volatility	0.015 [0.036]	–0.105 [0.042]**	0.017 [0.036]	–0.100 [0.038]***
(TOT growth) × (Exports/GDP)			–3.366 [2.093]	2.382 [0.897]***
Exports/GDP			–1.237 [4.424]	7.531 [3.811]*
Constant	1.154 [0.764]	3.119 [0.443]***	1.280 [0.824]	1.898 [0.700]***
Observations	79	125	79	125
R-squared	0.45	0.34	0.48	0.42
Mean Values (Standard Deviation)				
GDP growth	1.38 [1.28]	0.99 [1.79]	1.38 [1.28]	0.99 [1.79]
TOT growth	0.36 [1.09]	–0.49 [1.53]	0.36 [1.09]	–0.49 [1.53]
TOT volatility	7.67 [5.56]	9.46 [5.52]	7.67 [5.56]	9.46 [5.52]
(TOT growth) × (Exports/GDP)			0.03 [0.13]	–0.09 [0.35]
Exports/GDP			0.10 [0.06]	0.14 [0.12]
Marginal Impact				
TOT Trend growth	0.41	–0.04	0.41	–0.04
TOT Volatility	0.02	–0.11	0.02	–0.10
Impact of a 1 Standard Deviation Increase				
TOT Trend growth	0.45	–0.06	0.45	–0.06
TOT Volatility	0.08	–0.58	0.09	–0.55

Source: Blattman, Hwang and Williamson (2004), table 2.
Notes: Decade and country dummies used everywhere. Robust standard errors in brackets. *significant at 10%, **significant at 5%, ***significant at 1%.

(5)	(6)	(7)	(8)	(9)	(10)	(11)	(12)
1870–1909				1920–1939			
Core	Periphery	Core	Periphery	Core	Periphery	Core	Periphery
0.409 [0.141]***	−0.009 [0.147]	0.978 [0.307]***	−0.204 [0.147]	0.958 [0.484]*	−0.100 [0.306]	1.271 [0.997]	−0.309 [0.323]
0.071 [0.036]*	−0.109 [0.054]**	0.076 [0.036]**	−0.122 [0.049]**	0.001 [0.126]	−0.166 [0.126]	0.068 [0.184]	−0.155 [0.105]
		−7.489 [3.291]**	2.176 [0.995]**			−5.061 [4.024]	1.687 [1.520]
		7.165 [4.992]	15.361 [7.790]*			−10.444 [11.482]	10.358 [7.235]
0.498 [0.573]	3.42 [0.613]***	0.185 [0.605]	1.205 [1.048]	−1.052 [3.847]	2.079 [1.764]	−2.293 [4.647]	0.208 [1.892]
56	84	56	84	23	41	23	41
0.57	0.36	0.63	0.49	0.63	0.73	0.70	0.77
1.13 [0.76]	1.13 [1.70]	1.13 [0.76]	1.13 [1.70]	1.87 [1.85]	0.72 [1.96]	1.87 [1.85]	0.72 [1.96]
0.31 [0.86]	−0.01 [1.36]	0.31 [0.86]	−0.01 [1.36]	0.50 [1.54]	−1.48 [1.38]	0.50 [1.54]	−1.48 [1.38]
5.98 [3.91]	8.59 [5.63]	5.98 [3.91]	8.59 [5.63]	11.79 [6.80]	11.25 [4.90]	11.79 [6.80]	11.25 [4.90]
		0.03 [0.07]	0.00 [0.22]			0.03 [0.20]	−0.27 [0.48]
		0.09 [0.05]	0.13 [0.11]			0.11 [0.09]	0.16 [0.14]
0.41	−0.01	0.31	0.08	0.96	−0.10	0.70	−0.04
0.07	−0.11	0.08	−0.12	0.00	−0.17	0.07	−0.16
0.35	−0.01	0.27	0.11	1.47	−0.14	1.08	−0.05
0.28	−0.61	0.30	−0.69	0.01	−0.81	0.46	−0.76

The top half of table 6.2 reports the regression estimates and hypothesis testing for the terms-of-trade effects. The bottom half reports the quantitative and economic importance of these terms-of-trade effects. Thus, the bottom half shows the sample means and standard deviations of the independent variables, as well as their marginal impact. The latter is measured as the predicted change in output growth from a marginal increase in the independent variable. For terms-of-trade volatility, the marginal impact is just the coefficient estimate. Marginal impact is defined the same way for trend growth when there is no interaction term. When the interaction term is introduced, marginal impact is the sum of the coefficient estimates on TOT Trend Growth by itself and the interaction term, the latter multiplied by the mean export share. Finally, the last rows of table 6.2 show the predicted change in output from a one-standard-deviation increase in either the growth or volatility of the terms of trade, thus showing how a plausible change in either independent variable would have influenced output. The word "plausible" applies to the years covered by the sample, namely 1870–1939. The change may not be quite so plausible when applied outside the sample, namely 1820–1870, when the terms of trade for primary products soared, as we have seen in chapter 5. We return to this issue later.

Columns (1) and (2) strongly support the asymmetry hypothesis. Greater secular improvements in the terms of trade were significantly and positively associated with long-run output growth in the core, but not in the periphery. While the core benefited greatly from a small but positive secular improvement in its terms of trade, positive improvement in the periphery—when it made a rare appearance— did not translate in to more growth, but less. Greater volatility had a significant negative influence on income growth in the periphery, but not in the core. This asymmetry between core and periphery continues to hold when an interaction term between TOT Trend Growth and export share is introduced in columns (3) and (4). The net effect of trend growth will be sorted out later in the marginal impact calculations, but it is interesting to note the signs. The negative sign on the linear term for the periphery implies that terms-of-trade improvements reduced output growth there in that decade. However, the positive sign on the interaction term suggests that the negative effect was mitigated, perhaps entirely undone, by having a more open economy exporting a larger share of output.[10] An increase in export share, holding constant concentration, may have acted as a foil to rent-seekers, or exerted a positive influence on output growth through various channels, such as efficiency gains or the development of better institutions. Including the interaction term also improves the statistical significance on volatility.

The main findings continue to receive strong support for the pre–World War I years in columns (5) through (8). Secular improvements in the terms of trade raised long-run output growth in the core, but not in the periphery, while greater volatility diminished growth in the periphery, but not in the core. The interwar years—reported in columns (9) through (12)—involve a much smaller sample and, as a result, the standard errors are large and the statistical significance is low, but the point estimates are generally consistent with those found for the prewar era. It seems reasonable, therefore, to conclude that the same forces were at work both before and after the war.

The economic effects were very big. A one-standard-deviation increase in TOT Trend Growth was associated with a 0.45 percentage point increase in the average annual growth rate of per capita GDP—a big number given that the average annual per capita growth rate in the core was just 1.4 percent. The economic effect of TOT volatility in the periphery was even bigger—a one-standard-deviation increase lowered output growth by nearly 0.6 percentage points (the magnitudes being very similar with and without the interaction term). Moreover, when one channel of terms-of-trade impact is investigated—the flow of investment funds from Britain—it appears that capital inflows were negatively influenced by terms-of-trade volatility in the periphery, but not in the core (Blattman, Hwang, and Williamson 2004). To illustrate the impact of terms-of-trade volatility in the periphery, consider that per capita income in Canada grew faster than in Indonesia by about 1 percent per annum. The difference in terms of trade volatility between the two countries was just under one half of one standard deviation. The estimates in table 6.2 imply that if, through better luck in the commodity lottery, Indonesia had experienced Canada's smaller terms-of-trade volatility, then it would have grown faster by about 0.3 percentage points, reducing the growth rate gap between them by a third.

More generally, these magnitudes suggest that terms-of-trade shocks were an important force behind the big divergence in income levels between core and periphery, a core-periphery gap that started to open up so dramatically in the early nineteenth century (Pritchett 1997). The gap in growth rates in per capita income between core and periphery in our sample was 0.4 percentage points. If the periphery had experienced the same terms-of-trade volatility as the core (leaving the secular trend unchanged), 0.2 percentage points would have been added to average GDP per capita growth rates there. This alone erases half of the output per capita growth gap. If, in addition, the core had experienced no secular improvement in the terms of trade, instead of the observed 0.36 percent per annum growth rate, this would have reduced output growth there by 0.15 percentage points. Combined, these two counterfactuals would have eliminated nearly the entire gap in growth rates between core and periphery. Finally, these results are robust to the use of alternative periphery allocations, terms-of-trade growth and volatility measures, and time period.[11]

What accounts for the asymmetric terms of trade effects between core and periphery in the premodern era? The core benefited from a secular increase in its terms of trade since it reinforced comparative advantage there, helped stimulate industrialization, thus augmenting growth-induced spillovers. The fact that the periphery, in contrast, did not benefit when the terms of trade rose over the long-term, or suffer when it fell, appears to support deindustrialization and resource curse effects. But what accounts for the asymmetry between the core and periphery response to terms-of-trade volatility? Exactly what kind of insurance did the industrial core take out that allowed it to escape the damaging consequences of terms-of-trade instability, insurance that was not, apparently, available to primary-product exporters in the periphery? Did the industrial core simply have better-developed institutions, policies, and tax mechanisms by which to insure against adverse shocks? I do not offer any answers here in these lectures, but the questions certainly suggest an exciting agenda for the future.

Bucking the Global Tide with High Tariffs

How did the periphery respond to globalization-induced distributional events, to greater volatility, to deindustrialization, and to growth-suppressing forces? Was there antiglobal backlash periphery long before Import Substitution Industrial (ISI) policies became popular in the modern era? If so, what accounts for it? Where the autonomous periphery followed aggressive tariff policies, was the key motivation to mute global deindustrialization forces and soften the blow to import-competing industries? Or was it something else?

World Tariffs 1870–1938

Figure 7.1 reports the world ad valorem tariff rate averaged for our thirty-five countries,[1] in six regions of the world, since the 1860s: the United States; three members of the European industrial core (France, Germany, United Kingdom); three English-speaking European offshoots (Australia, Canada, New Zealand); ten from the industrially lagging European periphery (Austria-Hungary, Denmark, Greece, Italy, Norway, Portugal, Russia, Serbia, Spain, Sweden); ten from the Asian and the Middle Eastern

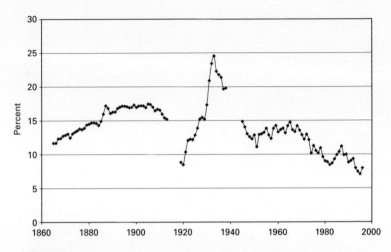

Figure 7.1
Unweighted world-average own tariff 1865–1997, 35 countries
Source: Williamson (2005: figure 1).

periphery (Burma, Ceylon, China, Egypt, India, Indonesia, Japan, the Philippines, Siam, Turkey); and eight from the Latin American periphery (Argentina, Brazil, Chile, Colombia, Cuba, Mexico, Peru, Uruguay). Figure 7.2 plots average tariff rates up to 1938 for the six regions.

Figures 7.1 and 7.2 document the well-known antiglobal surge to world protection in the 1920s and 1930s. What is much less well-known, however, is the persistent protectionist drift worldwide between 1865 and about 1900, a thirty-five-year drift sufficiently pronounced that tariffs were at least as high in 1900 as they were in 1938 everywhere in the periphery except Asia. What looks like a modest pre-World War I antiglobalization backlash in figure 7.1—a retreat from the liberal proglobal trade positions in midcentury (Williamson 1998; 2002a)—is far more dramatic when

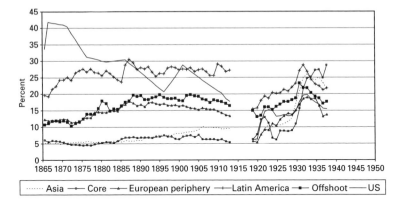

Figure 7.2
Unweighted average of regional tariffs before World War II
Source: Williamson (2005: figure 2).

the world averages are regionally disaggregated in figure 7.2. Indeed, there is a very pronounced and persistent secular rise in tariffs across Latin America, across the English-speaking European offshoots (the United States being the only exception) and across the European periphery. This steep rise up to the 1890s in the periphery's tariff rates (and their persistence at those high levels up to World War I) far exceeds that of the European core. This is an especially notable fact given that almost nothing has been written on this antiglobal trend in the periphery, while so much has been written about the far more modest backlash on the European continent (e.g., Gerschenkron 1943; Kindleberger 1951; Bairoch 1989).

In addition, note the enormous variance in levels of protection between the regional averages. The richer, new-world European offshoots had levels of protection almost three times that of the European core around the turn of the century. When the United States is shifted to the rich European offshoot club, the ratio of European offshoot tariffs to that of the core is more than three to one. To take another example, in 1925 the European periphery had tariffs about two-and-a-half times higher than those in the European industrial core. To take yet another example, in 1885 the poor but independent parts of Latin America (Brazil, Colombia, Mexico, and Peru) had tariffs almost five times higher than those in the poor and dependent parts of Asia (Burma, Ceylon, China, Egypt, India, Indonesia, and the Philippines), while the poor but independent parts of Asia (Siam, Turkey, and Japan) had tariff rates about the same as the poor but dependent parts of Asia. Of course, colonial status, lack of autonomy, and "unequal treaties" all played an important role in Asia, and we will want to control for that fact in what follows.

Furthermore, there was great variance within these regional clubs. In 1905, tariffs in Uruguay (the most protectionist land-abundant and labor-scarce country) were about two-and-a-half times those in Canada (the least protectionist land-abundant and labor-scarce country). In the same year, tariffs in Brazil and Colombia (the most protectionist poor but autonomous countries in Latin America) were almost ten times those in China and India (the least protectionist poor and nonautonomous countries in Asia). The same high–low range appeared within the industrial core (the United States five times the United Kingdom) and the European periphery (Russia six times Austria-Hungary, Portugal more than three times Italy). Between 1919 and 1938, the tariff variance between countries was about the same as the tariff variance over time, but between 1865 and 1914, the tariff variance between countries was more than twice that of the tariff variance over time. Thus, explaining differences in tariff policy between countries is at least as important as explaining changes in tariff policy over the eight decades after the 1860s, perhaps more so.

The difference between center and periphery is marked. Prior to World War I, tariffs were much higher in the rich European offshoots than anywhere else. Furthermore, and as I have already mentioned, they would have been even higher had I allocated to this club one of the most protectionist, the United States (which is allocated instead to the core).[2] The European members of the industrial core (France, Germany, United Kingdom) had the lowest tariffs, although the United States serves to raise the club average. Most members of the poor periphery in Asia were colonies or quasi-colonies of the industrial core (Burma, Ceylon, Egypt, India, Indonesia, and the Philippines), or were forced to sign free trade agreements ("unequal treaties") with the core in midcentury since the latter trained naval guns on their potential trading partners (China, Japan), or the former viewed nearby gunboats as a sufficient threat to go open on their own (Siam). Thus, tariff rates in Asia were pretty much like those of the core early on, but they started drifting upwards after the 1880s, when the unequal treaties had expired and long before the post–World War II independence movement.

I should also interject that colonial status did not necessarily imply lack of local influence on tariff policy. There are five colonies in our sample from Asia: Burma, Ceylon, India, Indonesia, and the Philippines, although foreign influence was strong enough (including occupation) to make Egypt behave like a colony. While colonial tariff policy did indeed mimic that of their masters, local conditions mattered as well (Clemens and Williamson 2002). For example, while India's ad valorem tariff rates were on average about the same as free-trading Britain, those of Burma and Ceylon were 4 or 5 percentage points higher, and those of Egypt were 10 points higher. Clearly, local conditions mattered even in colonies of the same colonist. But who the colonist was also mattered: tariff rates in the Philippines were unrelated to those in Spain before 1899, but very closely related to those in the United States after 1898. Thus, I retain the full Asian sample of ten in all that follows, although I will take care to control for colonial status and tariff autonomy.

There is plenty of evidence of rising world protection before World War I (the unweighted average in the full sample rising from about 12 percent in 1865 to about 17.5 percent in 1900), but much of that antiglobal reaction was centered in the periphery. Indeed, the much-studied European continental backlash plotted in figure 7.2 looks pretty modest compared with what happened in the periphery. The antiglobal backlash took place in the European English–speaking offshoots. While the United States retreated from its enormous Civil War tariffs, they remained the highest in the world for some time. Everywhere else in the English-speaking offshoots, tariffs rose between 1865 and 1900: Canada by about 3 percentage points; Australia by more than 7 percentage points; and New Zealand by almost 12 percentage points. The antiglobal surge in Latin America was led by Columbia (up almost 7 percentage points) and Uruguay (up more than 10 percentage points). The European periphery leaped to high levels of protection after the 1870s, with Russia leading the way. And while it had the lowest tariffs in 1865, even Asia had by 1914 raised them to levels that approached that of the protectionist English-speaking European offshoots.

It might be useful to summarize the three major surprises that these world tariff data document. First, and to repeat, the traditional literature has made much of the tariff back-lash on the European continent to the "grain invasion" from North America, Argentina, and Russia after the 1870s (Kindleberger 1951; Bairoch 1989; O'Rourke 1997). Between the 1870s and the 1890s, average tariff rates rose by 5.7 per-centage points in France (to 10.1 percent) and 5.3 percentage points in Germany (to 9.1 percent). However, this antiliberal move to higher tariffs by the leading economies on the con-tinent is repeated in the European periphery (up 4.2 per-centage points to 16.8 percent) and in our four poor Latin American countries (up 6.9 percentage points to 34 percent). The increase is no less dramatic and it results in far higher tariffs.

Second, the traditional literature teaches us that the Latin American reluctance to go open in the late twentieth-century was the product of the Great Depression and the import substitution industrial (ISI) strategies that arose in its wake (Diaz-Alejandro 1984; Corbo 1992). Yet, Latin America already had by far the highest tariffs in the world by the late-nineteenth century (Coatsworth and Williamson 2004a, 2004b). Thus, whatever explanation is offered for the Latin American commitment to high tariffs, it must search for origins well before the Great Depression.

Third, it is not true that Asia waited for post–World War II independence to switch to protectionist policies. I have already noted that there was an upward surge in tariff rates in Asia after the 1880s and early 1890s, illustrated best by Burma, India, the Philippines, Siam, and Turkey. With the exception of Egypt and Japan, all of the Asian countries underwent a surge to high tariffs in the 1930s, and most of these countries stuck with these higher tariffs into the 1940s and the modern era. Presumably, the surge in Asian tariffs from the 1880s to the 1930s was due to a weakening colonial grip and to the expiration of those "unequal treaties" signed decades earlier, both of which would have given the region the increasing autonomy to set higher tariffs had local political economy forces been pushing in that direction.

Tariffs took two big leaps upward in the interwar decades, and these took place worldwide. The first leap was in the 1920s, which might be interpreted as a return to high prewar tariffs. The second was in the 1930s, with its well-known and aggressive beggar-my-neighbor policies. The biggest interwar tariff hikes in the industrial core were initiated by Germany and the United Kingdom, but France and the United States were not far behind. All of this is well appreciated in the literature. What is not well appreciated, however, is that a big pre-1914 spread between the high-tariff autonomous periphery and the low-tariff industrial core completely evaporated in the interwar. That is, the core raised tariffs in the 1930s to levels that had been common in the periphery before World War I. Still, tariffs rose even higher in most of the European periphery and almost everywhere in Latin America, Asia, and the Middle East. This was especially true of the colonies in Asia. To give some sense of how large the rise in tariff barriers was around an Asian periphery dominated by allegedly passive and free-trading colonies, the ad valorem tariff rate rose in India by 22 percentage points between 1920 and 1939, in Egypt it rose by 36.7 percentage points between the same two years, in Siam it rose by 26.9 percentage points between 1918 and 1936, and in Turkey it rose by 34.1 percentage points between 1923 and 1937.

Was It Stolper-Samuelson?

Were the high and rising periphery tariffs before the modern era driven by some antiglobal reaction, that is, by some backlash? Until the race towards autarky in the 1930s, the free traders were members of the industrial core, their colonies, or those who had been intimidated by gunboats to open up. The rest had erected high tariff walls. Did the autonomous periphery exhibit global backlash? In the three decades or so following the 1850s, the rise in tariff rates was ubiquitous worldwide. Was this upsurge a backlash response to the spectacular fall in transport costs that was serving to integrate world commodity markets and to blow the winds of international competition down the necks of import-competing industries that geography had protected before? It is essential to get answers to these questions if the modern debate about the future of globalization is to be properly informed by history. Simply to show high and rising tariffs in the periphery is not enough. Did globalization backlash account for it?

The most elegant backlash explanation has its roots in the economics of Eli Heckscher and Bertil Ohlin, who told us how endowments could account for trade patterns, factor abundance dictating competitiveness in world markets and what would be exported by whom. More to the point, Heckscher (1919: reprinted in Flam and Flanders 1991) showed (in Swedish) how foreign trade affected the distribution of income, opening the way for Wolfgang Stolper and Paul Samuelson (1941) to elaborate the corollary (in English and mathematics), namely that the scarce factor should favor protection and the abundant factor should favor free trade. About fifteen years ago, Stolper-Samuelson thinking was used with great skill by Ronald Rogowski (1989) who applied it to country trade policy the world around from 1840 to the present. But there were two limitations to the way Rogowski used the Stolper-Samuelson corollary, and they matter. First, the corollary only tells us who votes for what, not who wins the voting. Since the landed elite dominated voting in land scarce Europe,[3] the import-competing sectors got the protection from foreign grains that the landed elite wanted. Trade theorists have, in fact, offered an explicit rule whereby the "equilibrium tariff increases with the square root of the ratio of the country's scarce factor to its abundant factor" (Magee, Brock, and Young 1989: 25). Alternatively, as the scarce factor shrinks in relative size, its power at the polls shrinks, too. However, what happens to such endowment rules when the scarce factor does not have the vote at all, as was true of labor throughout most of the world before the 1930s?[4] Did labor get the protection of import-competing manufacturing that it should have wanted in labor-scarce Latin America, in the labor-scarce English-speaking new world, and in labor-scarce southeast Asia? Second, Rogowski used the corollary to speak to levels of protection but not to changes in protection. We want to know whether a rise in protection can be attributed to globalization backlash and to compensation of the injured scarce factor. Thus, a dynamic version of Stolper-Samuelson is more relevant than a static version.

So, when the import-competing sector was injured by an adverse price shock—an improvement in the country's terms of trade induced by world market events or by declining seaborne transport costs that reduced import prices and raised export prices, was there always a compensation effect that drove up tariffs? The answer will depend in part on whether the factors in the slumping sector could escape by migrating to the booming sector. Of course, in general equilibrium the scarce factor cannot completely escape injury by emigrating from the import competing sector, since these effects leave their mark even economy-wide. But the mark is much smaller. Thus, Stolper-Samuelson economics has a far better chance of explaining nineteenth-century tariff policy when, after all, most trade was in primary products, and immobile specific factors—land and other natural resources—played such a big role. The more trade was dominated by immobile, sector-specific factors, the more would those factors complain when hit by unfavorable price shocks. Stolper-Samuelson economics has a much poorer chance of explaining modern tariff policy when, instead, trade is dominated by manufactures and most factors—labor, skills, and capital—are mobile.[5] Today, mobile factors can escape most of the trade-induced injury by fleeing the sector hit by bad price shocks.

Was It Infant Industry?

It has always been believed that development policy was a second powerful motivation for high tariffs on imported manufactures in the early-industrial periphery. Public authorities have been persuaded by two centuries of history that industrialization is the only vehicle for development. Those same authorities were persuaded for much of the twentieth century that protection was the only way to foster that process. Indeed, they often cited nineteenth-century experience to help support these claims. I will call this motivation "the infant-industry argument" for short, with the understanding that it includes development and industrial policy.

Does protection help or hinder growth? Presumably, it should be useful to see whether policymakers in the autonomous parts of the periphery could have used such evidence to support their protectionist policies in the century before the 1930s. Of course, policymakers of that time did not have the models, methods, and evidence that we can exploit today, but they certainly would have had the intuition. Were we asking this question about the late-twentieth century, then the evidence would strongly support the position that protection hindered growth. But what about the premodern era? Did protection foster[6] growth in the periphery before World War II when those tariffs were so high?

Policymakers in those parts of the periphery that had tariff autonomy were certainly aware of the pro-protectionist infant-industry argument offered for the German *Zollverein* by Frederich List and for the United States customs union by Alexander Hamilton. This was certainly true of late-nineteenth century Latin America (Bulmer-Thomas 1994: 140) and the European periphery. However, it is important to stress "late" in the previous sentence, since the use of protection specifically and consciously to foster industry does not occur in Mexico until the early 1890s, Brazil and Chile a little later in the 1890s, Colombia in the early 1900s (Márquez 2002; Coatsworth and Williamson 2004a, 2004b), and Tsarist Russia about the same time (Bairoch 1989). So, the evidence suggests that protection for industrial development becomes a significant motivation for tariffs in the periphery only near the turn of the previous century. In any case, there is absolutely no pre–World War I evidence from the periphery that would have supported infant industry arguments. Indeed, before 1914 high tariffs were correlated with slow growth in Latin America (Coatsworth and Williamson 2004a), just as it has been in the late-twentieth century developing world.[7]

We must look elsewhere for plausible explanations for the exceptionally high (and often rising) tariffs in the autonomous periphery in the century before the Great Depression. One of the alternative explanations that I will explore below involves the revenue needs of central governments. As a signal of things to come, I simply note here that the openness-growth causation probably went the other way round in the autonomous periphery. That is, countries achieving rapid GDP per capita growth also underwent faster growth in imports and in other parts of the tax base, thus reducing the need for high tariff rates, even to finance a growing government expenditure share. And countries suffering slow growth would have kept tariff rates high to ensure adequate revenues for government expenditure needs, and they would have raised those tariff rates if their intent was to increase their expenditure shares on infrastructure and other public goods.

The Political Economy of Tariffs: Some Preliminaries

Tariffs for Revenue

Were revenues a strong motive for high tariffs? If so, were those high premodern tariffs in the autonomous periphery really all that the market could bear? The revenue-maximizing tariff hinges crucially on the price elasticity of import demand. Tariff revenue can be expressed as $R = tpM$, where R is revenue, t is the average ad valorem tariff rate, p is the average import price, and M is import volume. Totally differentiating with respect to t, and assuming that the typical nineteenth-century country in the periphery was a price-taker for manufacturing imports, yields $dR/dt = pM + (tp)dM/dt$. The revenue-maximizing tariff rate, t^*, is found by setting $dR/dt = 0$ (the peak of some Laffer Curve), in which case $t^* = -1/(1 + \eta)$, where η is the price elasticity of demand for imports. Irwin (1998a: 14) estimates the price elasticity to have been about -2.6 for the United States between 1869 and 1913. Since the import mix for countries around the periphery was similar to that of the United States, taking the price elasticity for the former to have been around −3 can't be too far off the mark. Under those assumptions, the revenue-maximizing tariff in the autonomous periphery would have been very high indeed, about 50 percent.[8]

Alternatively, suppose some government in the periphery had in mind some target revenue share in GDP ($R/Y = r$) and could not rely on foreign capital inflows to balance the current account (so $pM = X$), then $r = tpM/Y = tX/Y$. Clearly, if foreign exchange earnings from exports (and thus imports) were booming (an event which could be caused either by a terms of trade boom, denoted here by a fall in the relative price of imports, p, or by a supply-side expansion that increased export quantities, X, or both), then the target revenue share could have been achieved at lower tariff rates, t. The bigger the export boom, the higher the export share, the bigger the import share, and the lower the necessary tariff rate.

Of course, countries in the periphery that were successful in getting external finance from the European core would have had less reason to use high tariffs to augment revenues in the short run and medium term. Since world capital markets became increasingly well integrated up to 1913 (Obstfeld and Taylor 2003), high tariffs that were necessary in 1865 would have been far less necessary in 1913 if "revenue smoothing" was a key motivation. However, there may have been plenty of motivation to raise them again when world capital markets fell apart in the interwar years. Furthermore, countries that developed internal (and less distortionary) tax sources would have had less need for high tariffs, an event that started in the late nineteenth-century industrial core, accelerating during the interwar rise of the welfare state (Lindert 1994, 2003). Such developments lagged way behind in the periphery, however.

So, did autonomous governments in Latin America, the European periphery and Asia act as if they were meeting revenue targets? Ceteris paribus, did they lower tariff rates during secular booms in primary product markets when their export shares were high and rising, and did they raise them during primary product slumps? Note that a terms-of-trade boom in the periphery had offsetting effects: as we have seen previously, motivation by revenue targets would have served to lower tariffs; as we see next, motivation by deindustrialization fears or Stolper-Samuelson compensation would have served to raise tariffs.

Stolper-Samuelson and Scarce Factor Compensation

The Stolper-Samuelson theorem tells us that protection benefits owners of factors in which that society is poorly endowed, that is, the scarce factors. According to this kind of thinking, capitalists in the autonomous periphery should have been looking to form protectionist coalitions as soon as the first global century began to threaten them with freer trade. They did not have far to look in Latin America, either because they managed to dominate oligarchic regimes that excluded other interests, or because they readily found coalition partners willing to help, or both (Rogowski 1989; Coatsworth and Williamson 2004a).

Why no scarce labor in the Latin American tale? Growth, peace, and political stability after the 1860s did not necessarily produce democratic inclusion in Latin America. Most countries in the region limited the franchise to a small minority of adult men until well into the twentieth century, and suffrage for the working man would come even later in the Asian and Middle Eastern periphery. Literacy and wealth requirements excluded, as we have seen, most potential voters in virtually every Latin American and Asian country (Engerman, Haber, and Sokoloff 2000). Thus, the premodern periphery tended to produce oligarchic governments in which those urban capitalists who were linked to external trade and finance played a dominant role. Free-trading landowners formed the second dominant part of the governing oligarchy in countries that specialized in exporting agricultural products, and the same was true of the Ottoman Empire, Siam, and other labor-scarce parts of the periphery that had autonomy. Free-trading mineral export interests usually had less direct leverage in governmental decision making, despite the size and significance of their investments. The protectionist interests that mattered were those in the import-competing sector, which meant manufacturing in most of the periphery.

To the extent that Stolper-Samuelson thinking is useful in accounting for the variance in tariff rates, we would expect plenty of regional differences, as Rogowski has argued. After all, very different endowments and political participation characterized various parts of the periphery. The land-abundant, English-speaking new world countries were places where scarce labor had a powerful political voice to lobby for protection, joining scarce capital. The European periphery had scarce land and capital lobbying for protection, while the voices of free-trading labor were suppressed. Southeast Asia had scarce labor and capital, but with political participation limited to free-trading landed and trading interests. The rest of Asia was pretty much land and capital scarce, but free-trading labor had little or no political voice. The important point here is that the Stolper-Samuelson theorem tells us who should vote for free trade and who should vote for protection, but it does not tell us who gets the most votes.

Deindustrialization Fears and Scarce Factor Compensation

Were high and rising tariffs in the periphery generated by deindustrialization fears and/or by Stolper-Samuelson compensation of injured scarce factors in response to falling import prices?

Three ingredients were essential to the survival of any import-competing industry in the periphery: low costs of inputs—like labor, power, and raw materials; high productivity in the use of those inputs; and high market prices of output. Policymakers in the periphery could not do much about the first two,[9] but they could do a great deal about the third by pushing up tariff barriers, excluding foreign imports and thus raising the domestic price of manufactures relative to other commodities produced for home or foreign markets. When industrial productivity advance in the core was fast, world prices of manufactures declined relative to other products, and foreign firms became increasingly competitive in local periphery markets. Thus, policymakers in the periphery who favored industry, and/or the scarce factors used there, had reason to raise tariffs in response to any sharp decline in the relative price of manu-factures in world markets, especially relative to prices of the primary products the periphery exported to the core. In short, if the periphery had deindustrialization fears, or wanted to compensate scarce factors damaged by foreign competition, it would have raised tariffs in response to falling prices of manufactures in world markets, and thus to an improvement in the periphery's terms of trade.

Evaporating Geographic Barriers and Scarce Factor Compensation

High transport costs on goods imported from one's trading partner are just as protective as high tariffs. When new transport technologies induced the dramatic fall in freight costs documented in lecture I, the winds of competition thus created must have given powerful incentives to import-competing industries (and scarce factors) to lobby for more protection. The nineteenth-century transport revolution (O'Rourke and Williamson 1999: chapter 3; Mohammed and Williamson 2004) gave plenty of incentive for manufacturing interests in the periphery and agricultural interests in the core to lobby for protection as the natural barriers afforded by transport costs melted away. This connection was confirmed long ago for the "invasion of grains" into Europe from Russia and overseas. But what about the "invasion of manufactures" into the periphery from industrial Europe and, eventually, the United States?

The transport revolution took many forms, but, as we have seen, two mattered most: a decline in overseas freight rates (aided by the appearance of major canals, like the Suez and the Panama), and the penetration of railroads into interior markets. Freight rates fell everywhere, but mainly on routes carrying high-bulk intermediates and foodstuffs to Europe, much less on routes carrying low-bulk manufactures to the periphery. Meanwhile, railroads penetrated everywhere, and this fact might have been especially relevant for tariff policy where markets were mainly located in the interior. If railroads exposed previously isolated interior local manufacturing to increased foreign competition, those interests should have lobbied for more protection, and railroad penetration of the interior was especially important in Latin America, eastern Europe, and even India.

Strategic Trade Policy, the Terms of Trade, and Tariffs

A well-developed theoretical literature on strategic trade policy predicts that nations have an incentive to inflate their own terms of trade by raising tariffs, unless, of course, trading partners agree to mutual concessions (e.g., Dixit 1987; Bagwell and Staiger 2002). According to this kind of thinking, a country's own tariffs will depend at least in part upon the country's external tariff environment. Elsewhere, a principal-trading-partners'-tariff index has been calculated for our thirty-five countries and it shows that in the two decades before World War I every region except the industrial core and Latin America faced much lower tariff rates in their main export markets than they themselves erected against competitors in their own markets (Blattman, Clemens, and Williamson 2002). The explanation, of course, is that their main export markets were located in the European core, where tariffs were much lower. Thus, most of the periphery faced much lower tariffs than did the core, although this was not true of Latin America for whom the protectionist United States was such an important market. During the interwar years there was convergence: tariff rates facing the periphery rose very steeply as the core made that big policy switch from free trade to protection; as a consequence, every regional club faced very similar and high tariff rates in their export markets by the end of the 1930s.

While the strategic trade policy thesis holds promise in helping account for higher tariffs in Latin America trading with the heavily protected United States, and in that part of the European periphery trading with more-protectionist France and Germany, it holds less promise for that part of the European periphery whose exports were sent to free-trading United Kingdom. Indeed, between 1900 and World War I a decline in partner tariffs took place everywhere in the periphery except in the European periphery, suggesting a leader-follower reaction that varied across the periphery depending on who the dominant trading partner was, e.g., an ultraprotectionist United States lowering tariffs, a moderately protectionist France and Germany raising tariffs, or a free trade Britain standing pat (Blattman, Clemens, and Williamson 2002).

Price Volatility and the Specific-Duty Effect

Inflations and deflations have had a powerful influence on average tariff rates. Import duties were typically specific until modern times, quoted as pesos per bale, yen per yard, or dollars per bag. Under specific duty regimes, abrupt changes in price levels serve to change import values in the denominator, but not the legislated duty in the numerator, thus producing big equivalent ad valorem or percentage tariff rate changes. This specific-duty effect implies, of course, that debating the tariff structure is politically expensive, and thus is only infrequently changed by new legislation. The specific-duty effect has been explored most fully for the United States (Crucini 1994; Irwin 1998b: 1017), but it has also been identified for Mexico (Márquez 2002: 307), and, more generally, for Latin America (Coatsworth and Williamson 2004a). The specific-duty effect has not, however, been explored at a global level. Nor does the literature tell us why specific duties seem to be much more common in young, nonindustrial, and poor countries. One answer might be this: Poor countries export primary products, concentrating on only a few, thus exposing themselves to greater price volatility, as we have seen in the previous chapter. Since export revenues and import expenditures are highly correlated, volatile export prices imply volatile export values and, finally, volatile tariff revenues. Specific duties in the periphery must have helped smooth out the impact of the export price instability on government finances. Another answer might be this: Honest and literate customs inspectors are scarce in poor countries, but they are essential for implementing an ad valorem tariff where import valuation is so crucial. So, legislators in the periphery may have imposed specific duties to minimize the "theft" of state tariff revenues by dishonest and illiterate customs agents.

Policy Packages and Real Exchange Rate Trade-Offs

Few policies are decided in isolation. Indeed, there were other ways that governments could have improved the competitive position of import-competing industries, if such protection was their goal, and they explored many of these alternatives in the 1930s and in the ISI years that followed. Yet, they clearly understood these alternatives even before World War I. One powerful alternative involved manipulating the real exchange rate. If governments chose to go on the gold standard or to peg to a core currency, they got more stable real exchange rates in return (and an attractive advertisement for foreign capital: Meissner 2004). However, since protection via real exchange rate manipulation was forgone, tariff rates would have to go up to reclaim that protection lost. Did countries exploit this trade-off both during the

years of gold standard commitment before World War
I and during the interwar years when everybody went off
gold?

The Political Economy of Tariffs: Empirical Analysis

The potential explanations for tariff policies discussed
before can be allocated to four main motives: revenue needs,
scarce factor tariff compensation, strategic trade policy, and
infant-industry arguments. I take the latter to be a modern
motivation, and I will ignore it in the premodern analysis
that follows. While the remaining three motives need not
have been competing, we would still like to know which
played the biggest roles, and in which periods and places.
Elsewhere, an econometric attack was launched on the
problem two ways (Blattman, Clemens, and Williamson
2002; Clemens and Williamson 2002; Coatsworth and
Williamson 2004a): first, by treating the experience as comparative world economic history and thus exploring time
series only (*TS*); and second, by exploring the cross-section
variance across these thirty-five countries using time fixed
effects (*CS*). The cross-section results are transformed to
remove serial correlation (using the *AR*(1) Cochrane-Orcutt
correction), and the time series are all estimated using
random effects (*RE*) after likewise correcting for serial correlation (with a Baltagi-Wu estimator). Table 7.1 presents the
time series and cross-section results. Each of these contains
various columns, necessitated by the fact that data coverage
for inflation and the terms of trade is inferior to that of the
other regressors. The right-hand side variables suggested by
the previous discussion are the following (all but dummies
in logs), allocated to the three central motives.

Revenue Motive

Lagged Export Share This export/GDP ratio is a measure of export boom, where we expect booms in the previous year to diminish the need for high tariff rates this year—if government revenues are a key motivation—thus yielding negative coefficients in the regression.[10]

Strategic Tariffs Motive

Lagged Partner Tariffs Strategic tariff policy suggests that countries should have imposed higher tariffs this year if they faced higher tariffs in their main markets abroad last year.

Stolper-Samuelson Scarce Factor Compensation Motive

Terms-of-Trade Index In the periphery, this terms-of-trade variable measures the price of each jth country's primary product exports (Pxj) relative to the price of manufactures (Pm) in world markets. In the core, the opposite is the case. If deindustrialization fears in the periphery were dominant, a positive coefficient should appear: price shocks in world markets that were good for the periphery's export sectors were bad for import-competing sectors, inviting compensation for the injured parties. Thus, the sign on the *ln(Lagged Px/Pm)* term should tell us whether deindustrialization fears dominated in the periphery. In the land-scarce European core and in land-scarce Asia (like Japan), imports were dominated by foodstuffs and raw materials. Here, Px/Pm speaks to an "invasion of grain" fear, whether wheat or rice, inviting compensation for the injured parties in this case too.

Table 7.1
Tariff Rate Determinants the World around 1870–1938
Dependent Variable: *ln* Own Tariff
Includes *AR*(1) Baltagi-Wu (*TS*) or Cochrane-Orcutt (*CS* serial correlation correction)

	TS, country *RE*			
Years Countries	1870–1938 All	1870–1938 All	1870–1938 All	1870–1938 All
Revenue Motive				
ln export share	−0.0285 (−1.36)	−0.0832 (−3.02)	−0.0609 (−2.30)	−0.0463 (−2.07)
Strategic Tariff Motive				
ln partner tariffs	0.2490 (9.06)	0.2507 (6.64)	0.2992 (8.45)	0.2246 (7.54)
Stolper-Samuelson Scarce Factor Compensation Motive				
ln terms-of-trade index				0.0798 (2.22)
ln GDP per capita	−0.1412 (−2.40)	−0.2227 (−2.86)	−0.1745 (−2.28)	−0.1810 (−2.95)
ln schooling	0.1640 (4.02)	−0.0560 (−0.82)	−0.0573 (−0.84)	0.1719 (4.30)
ln effective distance	−0.0735 (−4.86)	−0.1072 (−4.95)	−0.1267 (−5.97)	−0.0584 (−3.76)
ln railway mileage	0.0354 (3.38)	0.0639 (2.25)	0.0579 (1.98)	0.0347 (3.41)
ln urbanization	0.0478 (2.13)	0.0198 (0.30)	0.0013 (0.02)	0.0462 (2.10)
Controls				
ln population	−0.1084 (−2.50)	−0.1716 (−3.35)	−0.1441 (−2.81)	−0.1172 (−2.58)
Federal				
Colony				
Inflation			−0.0004 (−1.45)	
Inflation squared			0.0000 (2.45)	

CS, year dummies					
1870–1938 All	1870–1938 All	1870–1938 All	1870–1938 All	1870–1938 All	1870–1938 All
−0.0924 (−3.32)	−0.0397 (−1.37)	−0.0645 (−1.67)	−0.0601 (−1.60)	−0.0539 (−1.80)	−0.0753 (−2.02)
0.2526 (6.67)	−0.0440 (−1.22)	−0.0983 (−1.82)	−0.0338 (−0.60)	−0.0648 (−1.76)	−0.0953 (−1.73)
0.1219 (2.68)				0.1037 (2.55)	0.1371 (2.66)
−0.2260 (−2.90)	−0.1025 (−1.48)	−0.1445 (−1.44)	−0.1228 (−1.24)	−0.1439 (−2.00)	−0.1435 (−1.45)
−0.0416 (−0.61)	0.0672 (1.49)	−0.3046 (−2.96)	−0.2993 (−3.01)	0.0548 (1.22)	−0.3053 (−2.99)
−0.1086 (−5.02)	−0.0169 (−0.74)	−0.0644 (−1.53)	−0.0514 (−1.28)	−0.0309 (−1.29)	−0.0616 (−1.48)
0.0590 (2.08)	0.0055 (0.80)	0.0212 (0.93)	0.0190 (0.84)	0.0042 (0.56)	0.0219 (0.94)
0.0235 (0.36)	0.0242 (0.99)	−0.0890 (−1.58)	−0.0989 (−1.66)	0.0211 (0.79)	−0.0787 (−1.41)
−0.1721 (−3.38)	−0.1224 (−2.85)	−0.0433 (−0.84)	−0.0545 (−1.12)	−0.1302 (−3.00)	−0.0504 (1.00)
	0.0100 (0.35)	0.0524 (1.45)	0.0585 (1.55)	0.0071 (0.25)	0.0509 (1.35)
	−0.0033 (−0.05)	−0.1649 (−0.83)	−0.2797 (−1.58)	−0.0695 (−1.50)	−0.1515 (−0.79)
−0.0005 (−1.46)			−0.0004 (−0.90)		−0.0003 (−0.69)
0.0000 (1.77)			0.0000 (0.44)		0.0000 (0.52)

Table 7.1
(continued)

| | TS, country RE | | | |
Years Countries	1870–1938 All	1870–1938 All	1870–1938 All	1870–1938 All
Constant	2.7797 (4.75)	5.8022 (7.80)	5.4237 (7.45)	2.6333 (4.28)
N	2,138	1,169	1,300	1,951
Groups	35	30	35	35
Average observation/group	61.1	39	37.1	55.7
R-squared overall	0.224	0.271	0.25	0.251
DW original	0.222	0.242	0.251	0.227
DW transformed				

Source: Williamson (2005), table 1.
Notes: t-statistics are in parentheses below each coefficient estimate. War years (1914–1918) omitted.

Effective Seaborne Distance The distance from each country to either the United States or the United Kingdom (depending on trade volume), adjusted by seaborne freight rates specific to that route (Mohammed and Williamson 2004). If protection was the goal, effective distance should have served as a substitute for tariffs, so the regression should yield a negative coefficient.

Railway Mileage Added in kilometers. Poor overland transport connections from ports to interior markets served as a protective device for local manufacturing. Railroads reduced that protection, requiring higher tariffs to offset the effect. Thus, the regression should yield a positive coefficient.

	CS, year dummies				
1870–1938 All	1870–1938 All	1870–1938 All	1870–1938 All	1870–1938 All	1870–1938 All
5.1674 (6.68)					
1,169 30 39	2,067	1,116	1,238	1,889	1,116
0.266 0.245	0.144 0.083 1.972	0.203 0.107 1.979	0.195 0.115 1.948	0.149 0.083 1.982	0.211 0.111 1.987

GDP per Capita and Schooling   The latter referring to the primary school enrollment rate. These variables are taken as proxies for skill endowments, with the expectation that the more abundant the skills, the more competitive the industrial sector, and the less the need for protection, thus yielding a negative coefficient in the regression.

Urbanization   Taken as share of population in cities and towns greater than 20,000. This urbanization statistic is taken to be a Stolper-Samuelson proxy for the lobbying power of urban capitalists and artisans in the periphery, thus yielding a positive coefficient in the periphery regressions.[11]

Controls

Inflation   To the extent that countries used specific duties, inflation should have lowered tariff rates, thus yielding a negative coefficient. However, very rapid inflation might well have triggered a speedier legislative reaction with increases in specific duties, thus yielding a positive and off-setting coefficient on the squared term in the regression;

Population   Large countries have bigger domestic markets in which it is easier for local firms to find a spatial niche. Alternatively, bigger populations imply higher density, a fact that makes domestic tax collection easier and tariff revenues less necessary. In either case, the demand for protection should be lower in large countries, and the regression should produce a negative coefficient;

Federal   A dummy variable; if a federal system = 1, if centralized = 0. Federal governments had a stronger need for customs duties (since joining members usually retained most of their tax authority), while centralized governments could better exploit internal revenue sources. Thus, the regression should report a positive coefficient;

Colony   A dummy variable; if a colony = 1, 0 otherwise. With the exception of the Philippines, the colonies in our sample were controlled by free-trading colonialists (Britain and the Netherlands), implying a negative coefficient on the dummy variable.[12]

Comparative Tariff History Results

Turning first to the time series in table 7.1, we see that all coefficients have the expected sign with the exception of schooling (at least some of the time). Revenue motivation is revealed since export booms were associated with lower tariff rates. Global backlash and compensation forces are revealed too, and in many ways. A decrease in overseas transportation costs was associated with an offsetting rise in tariff barriers, and an increase in the length of the domestic rail network was associated with a symmetric rise in tariffs. As geographic barriers evaporated, import-competing industries were compensated by higher tariffs. Also, an improvement in a country's terms of trade in world markets generated a strong antiglobal reaction. For the periphery, this took the form of a deindustrialization reaction since an improvement in the relative price of their primary-product export in world markets implied a fall in the relative price of imported manufactures, inviting a tariff-raising lobbying reaction by industrial interests at home. For the European core, this took the form of a grain invasion reaction, as a rise in the relative price of their manufacturing exports implied a fall in the relative price of their imported foodstuffs, inviting a tariff-raising lobbying reaction by landed interests at home.

There is strong support for strategic tariff motives, since partner tariffs has a positive and significant coefficient throughout. The results for both schooling and urbanization depend on whether we control for inflation or not. Since including inflation reduces the sample size by almost half, however, we do not know if the different results for schooling and urbanization are due to the smaller sample or to the fact of controlling for inflation. In the full sample, an increase in urbanization was associated with an increase in tariffs, just as the Stolper-Samuelson theorem would predict, at least in the capital scarce periphery. Tariff rates fell with increases in GDP per capita, a result consistent with modern surveys of global attitudes (Mayda and Rodrik 2001;

O'Rourke and Sinnott 2001) but that can also be viewed as consistent with the Stolper-Samuelson theorem. Internal market size mattered in the predicted way: large countries had lower tariff rates. Finally, note that inflation had the predicted effect throughout the period, but that it was not statistically significant. More to the point, while inflation lowered tariff rates during wartime as predicted (figure 7.1), it did not do so during peacetime, at least in the restricted sample.

So much for statistical significance. What about historical significance? Why were tariffs on the rise nearly everywhere in the decades before 1900, especially in the autonomous periphery? Elsewhere, it has been shown that growing GDP per capita and population size were serving to lower tariffs everywhere, but these were overwhelmed by countervailing tariff-raising forces (Blattman, Clemens, and Williamson 2002). The push for higher tariffs came mostly from two sources: first, domestic political economy forces associated with urbanization and schooling; and second, a protectionist reaction serving to compensate import-competing industries as openness was thrust upon them by advances in transportation technology (both on land and sea). Only in the European periphery do we observe partner tariffs making a major contribution to the antiglobal, tariff-raising dynamics before 1900. Falling transportation costs certainly did contribute to rising tariff barriers in the European core, in the English-speaking European offshoots and in Asia. Yet, transport revolutions along the sea lanes had little impact on tariffs in Latin America and the European periphery, simply because the fall in overseas freight rates, and its impact, was more modest there. In addition, there is strong evidence of deindustrialization fears in the periphery, joining grain invasion fears in the core.

Overall, it appears to have been rising levels of railway penetration, schooling, urbanization (associated with changes in domestic politics), and improving terms of trade (at least up to the 1890s) that drove tariffs upwards in the premodern periphery. While the revenue motive was not a dominant force over the full seven decades after 1870, elsewhere it has been shown that it was a dominant force before (Coatsworth and Williamson 2004a, 2004b).

For the period from the 1890s to World War I, those antiglobal domestic political economy and (dissipating) transportation forces pushing tariffs upwards were finally overwhelmed by surging proglobal forces. Falling tariffs are associated with rising per capita incomes in Europe, their English-speaking and Latin American offshoots, the latter two carried in large part by mass immigrations and capital imports. The terms of trade effect was still operative, but now in a proglobal way yielding falling tariffs. That is, as the long run deterioration in the relative price of primary products started after the 1890s, the relative rise in the price of imported foreign manufactures eased the competitive pressure on local industry in the periphery. The upward pressure on tariffs also eased since there were fewer injured parties to compensate.

During the interwar decades, the increase in periphery tariffs were driven almost entirely by a "strategic tariff" reaction to the massive increase in core tariffs, a reaction that eclipsed all other tariff-setting forces.

Cross-Country Results

Now consider the cross-country results in table 7.1. Here we control for two additional characteristics: colonial status—an indicator of autonomy over tariff policy; and federal status—an indicator of the decentralization of governance.

Most of the tariff-setting forces identified in the comparative time series are confirmed in the cross-country analysis. However, three variables appear to have a different impact in the cross-section: partner tariffs, schooling, and urbanization. The partner tariffs variable is not significant in cross-section and appears to be negative. How can this be consistent with a world in which, as we have seen, changes in a country's own tariff is closely associated with changes in its trading partners' tariffs? This cross-sectional pattern suggests that initial conditions were such that, before reacting to changes in their partners' tariffs, countries began from a distribution in which its own high tariffs just happened for other reasons to be associated with low partner tariffs and vice versa. This pattern would appear to fit Asia's initial conditions at the dawn of the twentieth century: their own tariffs had been forced to be low, either as colonies or as victims of gunboat diplomacy, while high tariffs prevailed in their American and European trading partners. The European periphery would appear to fit this characterization, too: their backlash before World War I left them with high tariffs at a time when their trading partners in the European core had recently moved toward freer trade. This shows up in time series as a positive coefficient on trading partner tariffs, but the initial distribution of tariffs shows up in cross-section as a negative coefficient. A similar argument can explain the predominantly negative (but insignificant) cross-sectional coefficient on urbanization. I have no explanation for the nonrobust coefficients on the schooling variable. Still, the revenue and the Stolper–Samuelson scarce factor compensation motives are confirmed again in the cross-section.

What about historical significance? Why were tariffs so low before 1914 across Asia, the Middle East, and the European core? For Asia and the Middle East, lack of autonomy and the fact that the colonists were free-traders, mattered. Yet, those regions still obeyed the same political economy forces that prevailed in autonomous regions. One such force was the large internal markets in these labor rich and land scarce economies: bigger colonies had bigger internal markets in which local industry could find niches and thus had less need for protective tariffs. In the European core, an additional factor was industrial competitiveness, as captured by GDP per capita. Why were tariffs so high in both the Latin and English-speaking European offshoots? It appears that smaller domestic markets there made it harder for manufacturing firms to survive in a niche without walls to protect them, and, of course, they were less competitive since labor was relatively expensive. While the revenue motive was certainly present, and while the signs and magnitudes on the export share coefficient are the same in cross-section and time series, its influence is less powerful in the cross-section, a result I find surprising.

Dealing with Global Shocks in the Premodern Periphery

While surveying the political economy of trade policy a decade ago, Dani Rodrik concluded that the "links between the empirical and theoretical work have never been too strong" (Rodrik 1995: 1480). It appears that the boom in endogenous tariff theory over the past two decades has far outstripped the evidence brought to bear on it. Hopefully, the comparative tariff history on the premodern periphery reported here will help redress the balance.

While tariff policy for industrial Europe and the United States has been studied extensively, the rest of the world has not, and the majority, twenty-eight, of our sample of thirty-five countries are from the periphery: ten are from the European periphery; another ten are from Asia and the Middle East; and the remaining eight are from Latin America. What were the underlying fundamentals driving tariff policy in core and periphery? I think these questions should be at the top of the international economist's agenda. After all, even if we see high and rising tariffs in history, we need to know why they were high and rising if this history is to be used to understand the future of globalization in the present century.

We have learned a lot in this chapter. Revenue needs were an important determinant of tariff rates in the periphery before the 1870s, and especially for young republics with limited tax bases and limited access to foreign capital. As world capital markets improved after 1870, and as periphery governments broadened their tax bases, revenue needs gradually lost their influence on tariff setting. Thus, our empirical analysis, covering the full seven decades (1870–1938) or even just covering the decades before World War I (1870–1910), fails to find significant evidence that revenue needs still determined tariff rates in any ubiquitous and systematic way. Deindustrialization fears were a major determinant of tariff policy in the periphery before World War I, especially before the 1890s when the relative price of manufacturing imports underwent almost a century of dramatic secular decline. After the 1860s, grain-invasion fears in the European core joined deindustrialization fears in the periphery (which had been pronounced at least since the 1820s). Geography mattered, so that where and when the natural protection of distance and topography was conquered by transport technology, tariffs rose to compensate the injured import-competing industries. Finally, there was strategic tariff behavior at work everywhere after World War I, as countries with market power in both core and periphery tried to twist the terms of trade in their favor, thus reducing the gains from trade for all.

8   Coda: Some Guarded Lessons from History

What does premodern history tell us about the impact of globalization on the periphery?

In sharp contrast with the second global century since 1950, history shows that world market integration before World War I was driven entirely by a worldwide transport revolution on land and sea that served to erase geographic barriers to trade and to integrate previously isolated places with the global economy, whether they liked it or not. The autonomous periphery did not like it, and thus took an antiglobal stance manifested by high and rising tariffs. Since 1950, most of the globalization we observe has been driven instead by proglobal policy, rather than by transport revolutions. Modern globalization has moved along both an intensive margin—most countries have adopted increasingly proglobal policies over time—and an extensive margin—more and more countries have joined the proglobal club over time.

History also shows with great clarity how world globalization and differential rates of country-specific technical progress between core and periphery were both at work in a spectacular way during the 150 years before World War II. They produced two very distinct trends. First, there was

absolute factor price divergence between core and periphery, a rate of divergence greater than at any time in the
history of the world economy. GDP per capita, real wage,
and living standard gaps between core and periphery rose
from modest to immense levels between 1800 and 1940. This
absolute factor price divergence was driven by differential
rates of technical progress, and associated differential rates
of physical and human capital deepening, rates favoring the
core and disfavoring the periphery. We give this historical
event a name: the Industrial Revolution. Second, history
also generated relative factor price convergence within the
core, within the periphery, and between core and periphery.
This worldwide relative factor price convergence was manifested mostly by the convergence of the ratio of the wage
to land and resource rents as labor-abundant and land-
(resource) scarce economies became more like labor-scarce
and land-(resource) abundant economies, and vice versa.
Since global capital markets were by comparison well integrated, rates of return to financial assets were not a major
part of this relative factor price convergence. Nor was the
premium on skills a major part of this relative factor price
convergence, since human capital was not yet the important
factor of production that characterizes most economies
today. This relative factor price convergence was driven by
the forces of globalization—commodity price convergence,
booming trade, and mass migration.

In addition, history shows that the periphery's terms of
trade underwent spectacular secular change over the 150
years, tracing out a long cycle of boom and bust, with the
peak lying somewhere between the 1860s and 1890s, the
timing depending on the economy and its commodity
export specialization. Observers writing at the start of the
modern era—like Raúl Prebisch and Hans Singer, who con-

cluded that the relative price of primary-products (and thus the terms of trade for primary-product exporters) had fallen and would continue to fall, only looked at the downside of this 150-year cycle. This terms-of-trade experience was preceded by an even more dramatic secular improvement. This cycle obeyed standard laws of economic motion, driven both by transport revolutions and by the relative pace of technical progress and accumulation in world manufacturing.

Finally, history shows that the terms of trade had a powerful asymmetric growth impact on core and periphery. Where there was a secular improvement in the terms of trade, the core got a positive kick to long-run growth, but the periphery did not. This asymmetry is consistent with any theory that exploits an industry-carries-growth view. When the core enjoyed an improvement in its terms of trade, it got both a short-term income gain and a long-term stimulus to manufacturing, its export sector. When the periphery enjoyed an improvement in its terms of trade, it got the same short-term income gain but a long-term loss since manufacturing, its import-competing sector, was suppressed. Long-run de-industrialization losses swamped short-run income and specialization gains. In addition, there was far greater price volatility attached to primary products than to manufactures, so the periphery also faced a far more unstable world. Poor governments, poor firms, and poor households in the poor periphery could not insure against this instability as easily or as cheaply as could rich governments, rich firms, and rich households in the core or in the rich periphery (where the English-speaking settlers resided). Thus, price instability had a powerful asymmetric growth impact: it slowed down long-run growth in the poor periphery, while it had no effect on those parts of the core and the rich periphery that exported primary products.

These are powerful lessons of history, but should we expect them to carry over to the present? Maybe, maybe not. While I admit that "maybe" sounds like standard academic hedging to the question, I can be completely unequivocal in stating exactly what will influence the answer.

The relative factor price and thus income distribution impact of globalization was huge in the premodern periphery. Furthermore, it had a profound political impact. Inequality rose in the English-speaking overseas countries, while they absorbed unskilled labor and as their booming export sectors raised the rent on land and natural resources relative to unskilled labor's wage. These forces helped erase economic egalitarianism in the English-speaking overseas countries, and, given that the scarce factor (labor) already had the vote, created a globalization backlash there. Inequality fell in the European core, as emigration reduced an unskilled labor glut, as booming labor-intensive export sectors also raised wages, and as the grain invasion lowered land rents. These forces helped the working class get the vote, and thus served to improve their chances for implementing the welfare state. Rising inequality in resource abundant Latin America, where inequality was already very extensive and where the vote was limited to the wealthy few, served to inhibit political liberalism. Falling inequality in resource scarce East Asia served to accelerate political liberalism there.

But this premodern era was dominated by land and labor, and only the latter was mobile within any given economy. Thus, the external price shocks generated by globalization had its biggest impact on rewards to immobile land and other natural resources, factors of production whose rents collapsed when their terms of trade fell (since it was almost impossible for resources to migrate out of slumping sectors), and factors whose rents soared when their terms of trade rose (since it was almost impossible for additional resources to flow into the favored sector thus taking away those fat rents). In the modern era, land and natural resources are much less important while skills are much more important. Thus, since a dominant immobile factor in the past—land, has been replaced by a dominant mobile factor in the present—skills, the within-country impact of globalization on relative factor prices and income distribution is much less important today than it was a century ago. It follows that Stolper-Samuelson reactions to globalization shocks should be more modest today than they were a century ago.

Furthermore, while the periphery specialized in primary products in the premodern era, it now specializes in labor-intensive manufacturers. As we have seen, this regime shift has been relatively recent and dramatic: primary products as a share of Third World commodity exports fell from 85 to 18 percent between 1965 and 1998, while the share of manufactures rose from 15 to 82 percent. Much of the Third World is now relatively abundant in literate, low-skilled, urban labor, not natural resources, so it exports labor-intensive manufactures. Thus, positive terms of trade shocks and the growth of trade now helps it industrialize. The premodern terms of trade asymmetry between core and periphery has disappeared from most of the world, with only a residual left in the most premodern places, like Africa. The international economic order established in the first global century has been replaced by a new international economic order in the second global century.

All of this suggests that the powerful antiglobal reaction observed in the autonomous premodern and post–World War II developing periphery is far less likely to be observed in the twenty-first century.

Notes

Chapter 2

This section draws heavily on Williamson (2002b), Bértola and Williamson (2005), Mohammed and Williamson (2004), and Hatton and Williamson (2006: chapter 3).

1. Recent work has been able to uncover little or no evidence of commodity price convergence between Europe and Asia in the three centuries after 1500. The big globalization turning point was the 1820s (O'Rourke and Williamson 2002a, 2002b), after which commodity price convergence was dramatic, as we shall see later.

2. The "tyranny of distance" was the apt phrase that Geoffrey Blainey (1966/1982) used to describe its importance to Australian development.

3. Export shares in GDP were only 3.4 percent for Asia in 1913, but 25 percent for Latin America and 20 percent for Africa and Egypt combined (Blattman, Hwang, and Williamson 2004: table 1).

4. See also Gallup, Gaviria, and Lora (2003: 47–50). Of course, there were other factors at work too, like institutions, demography, slavery and luck in world commodity markets. But many of these were themselves influenced by geography.

5. At the end of lecture II, I make an overall assessment of the lessons of history. There I will stress how changes in economic environment dictate whether lessons can be transferred from the past to the present. Here is one example. Before 1800, natural resources can be taken as an endowment. After 2000, most natural resources cannot be taken as endowments since the two-century fall in transportation costs now makes it possible for coal

and oil scarce economies to import the stuff at little disadvantage in fuel costs. The same can be said today of arable land and foodstuffs, forests and wood products, iron deposits and steel production, and so on.

6. According to Maddison (2002: 127), it rose in Asia from 3.4 to 4.2 percent.

7. The calculations are based on an unweighted average of the growth rates of industrial production reported for France and the United Kingdom 1820–1850, and for France, Germany, and the United Kingdom 1850–1938 (Mitchell 1978: 179–183). The slowdown during 1820–1913 is bigger if the calculation is limited to only France and the United Kingdom, while it is smaller if the United States is added.

Chapter 3

This section draws heavily on Williamson (2002b), and O'Rourke and Williamson (2002a, 2002b, 2005).

1. "Agriculture" here excludes mining. Elsewhere in these lectures, however, primary products include output from both agriculture and mining.

2. The land-abundant and land-scarce averages in table 3.1 are across countries within the relevant regions, not across the regional averages.

3. How one allocates the Southern Cone matters here. See Williamson (2002b: table 2).

4. Maddison (1995: table 3–1, 60) reports "world" GDP per annum growth declining from 2.1 percent in 1870–1913 to 1.9 percent in 1913–1950. We have already reported similar figures for industrial production in the core.

Chapter 4

1. This question was pursued subsequently by, among others, Green and Urquhart (1976), Edelstein (1982), O'Rourke and Williamson (1999: chapters 11 and 12) and Clemens and Williamson (2004a).

2. This question was pursued subsequently by, among others, Findlay (1995) and Hatton and Williamson (1998, 2006).

3. As I argue in the text, where agriculture is "big" in preindustrial economies, the changing wage-rental ratio can be a very effective proxy for

trends in inequality. Although these lectures do not stress this point, the argument and evidence for it can be found in Williamson (1997, 1998, 2000, 2002a) and Lindert and Williamson (2003). By a "big" agriculture, I mean both one in which the share of agricultural land in total economy-wide tangible wealth is more than a third and/or in which the agricultural employment share is more than a half. Around the turn of the last century, when the agriculture employment share was 12 percent in Britain, and 24.7 percent in the combination of Britain, Germany, and the Netherlands (Mitchell 1998a: 150–160), it was about three times that in the periphery: Egypt 69.6, India 67.3, Indonesia 73.1, Japan 70, Taiwan 70.3, and Turkey 81.6 (Mitchell 1998b: 91–101); Mexico 71.9 (Mitchell 1993: 101); Portugal 66.9 and Spain 70.2 (Mitchell 1998a: 155–157). Another way to illustrate the difference between center and periphery is to compare the share of primary product exports in total exports. For the years 1905–1914, the average share for France, Germany, and Great Britain was 29.5 percent, while it was more than three times as big for Burma, Egypt, India, and Siam (91 percent).

4. Goldsmith (1985: table 40, 123) reports the share of agricultural land in tangible national wealth around World War I. The figures (in percent) were: Britain 9.9 and the United States 19.2, for an average of 14.5 for these two leaders in the industrial core; Japan 29.7, Mexico 23, and Italy 33.3, for an average of 28.7 for these three industrial followers in the periphery. Around 1850, the shares were much bigger, but Goldsmith offers fewer observations: Britain 19.9, the United States 35.8, and Italy 41.8. Presumably, the shares were even bigger in much of the (undocumented) primary-product oriented periphery. If livestock are added to agricultural land, the shares are bigger still. For example, the 1913 U.S. share increases from 19.2 to 22.7 percent (Goldsmith 1985: 18). The addition of farm structures and commodity inventories would raise the shares still further.

5. The data underlying figure 4.1 are taken from Yasuba (1996: table 2, geometrically interpolating between his benchmark observations for 1857, 1865, and 1875), and linked to the annual series in Yamazawa (1975: 539).

6. The arithmetic is simple enough. Let national income (Y) equal the sum of wages (wL, the wage per worker times the total labor force) and land rents (rD, rent per hectare times total hectares), and ignore skills, capital, and all else: $Y = wL + rD$. Then, per worker income growth is (where an "*" refers to the percentage growth over the fifteen or twenty years after 1858):

$$Y^* - L^* = w^*\theta_w + L^*(\theta_w - 1) + r^*\theta_r.$$

I assume that the share of income accruing to labor (θ_w) and land (θ_r) exhausted national income, and that land got 40 percent. (See note 7, where the land share in the 1880s is estimated by Hayami as about 37 percent, close to the 40 percent assumed here.) I also assume that land hectarage was fixed, and that labor force growth (assumed equal to population growth) was 7.6 percent between 1850 and 1870 (Maddison 1995: 106). If some of the GDP per capita growth between 1820 and 1870 actually took place before 1850, then land rents fell by even more than what I guess here. If the wage actually rose by less than Huber estimates, then land rents per hectare also rose by less, but the big wage-rental ratio rise would have been much the same.

7. The figure for 1883–1892, the earliest estimate available for agriculture in Japan, was 36.7 percent (Hayami 1975: table 2–11, 36, land rent as a share in the sum of land rent plus wages, the latter including imputed wages).

8. Chaudhuri (1983), Tomlinson (1993), and Whitcombe (1983). It is relative endowments that count for specialization and trade. Presumably, both labor and land had low productivity in the Punjab compared with Western Europe. The effective stocks of labor and land were both very low, accounting for low per capita income.

9. As this book was heading to press, I became aware of similar evidence for New Zealand (Greasley and Oxley 2004: 18, 23–24), where the wage-rental ratio also fell by 69 percent, in this case between 1873 and 1913. I should add that evidence on trends in land prices are often used to proxy trends in land rents, as is true in the New Zealand case.

10. Urbanization data are ubiquitous and accurate across countries, and their use as a proxy for industrialization and development has a very long tradition among economists. For recent examples, see DeLong and Shleifer (1993) and Acemoglu, Johnson, and Robinson (2001, 2002, 2003).

11. These south–south labor migrations within the poor periphery were as "mass" as were the north–north migrations within the Atlantic economy (Lewis 1978; Hatton and Williamson 2006: chapter 7), most of it involving emigration from labor-abundant India and China to labor-scarce Manchuria, Southeast Asia, the Indian Ocean, East Africa, the Caribbean, Queensland, the Pacific Islands, and elsewhere.

12. This is supported by a venerable tradition in Anglo-American economic history (Habakkuk 1962; David 1975) that has found recent empirical support in an even broader sample (O'Rourke, Taylor, and Williamson 1996).

Chapter 5

This chapter draws heavily on Clingingsmith and Williamson (2004).

1. The percent age of industrial workers who were spinners fell from 82 to 15 percent between 1809–1813 and 1901.

2. Most economists believe that industry generates accumulation and productivity externalities that agriculture does not, and thus that more industrialization generates more growth. The literature is extensive, but see, for example, Lewis (1954) and Murphy, Vishny, and Shleifer (1989).

3. Although they tend to be ignored in the historical deindustrialization literature, nontradables have always been central to Dutch disease models ever since Corden introduced them in the 1980s (Corden 1981, 1984; Corden and Neary 1982).

4. Parliamentary legislation made it necessary for colonial and foreign products to enter British ports before they could be re-exported to other markets. In 1772, reexports were about 61 percent of domestic exports from Britain and about 46 percent of imports (Mitchell and Deane 1962: 281).

5. To make matters worse, India, which had captured a good share of the English market in the seventeenth century, had—as an English defensive response—already been legislated out of that market by Parliamentary decree between 1701 and 1722 (Inikori 2002: 431–432), thus protecting local textile producers. But Parliament kept the Atlantic economy as a competitive free trade zone. Of course, the large Indian Ocean market was also a free trade zone, and India had dominated this for centuries (Chaudhuri 1978; Landes 1998: 154).

6. In the eighteenth century, these primary product exports were mainly indigo, raw silk, raw cotton, salt peter, and sugar. In the nineteenth century, jute, tea, and opium were added to the list in a big way.

7. If Indian data were available for 1705–1765, I think they would extend these trends backwards. After all, in England Pt/Pg declined only modestly between 1705 and 1765, and w/Pt hardly changed at all. My guess is that Pt/Pg fell sharply in India given that Pg about doubled between 1704–1706 and 1764–1766.

8. For example, there appears to be only one exception in the Ottoman economic history literature, that of Şevket Pamuk (1987). I have found no exceptions in the Indian economic history literature.

Chapter 6

This section draws heavily on Hadass and Williamson (2003), and Blattman, Hwang, and Williamson (2004).

1. It must be said that Prebisch, Singer, and much of the subsequent literature dealt with the relative price of primary products, not with the terms of trade facing any given country. Nor did they assess impact; rather, they assumed it.

2. Industrial manufactures have been a rapidly rising share of Third World output and exports. For example, for all developing countries, manufactures rose from only 17.4 percent of commodity exports in 1970 to 64.3 percent by 1994. Enough of the Third World is now labor-abundant and natural resource–scarce so that a fall in the relative price of primary products helps it to industrialize. The classic image of Third World specialization in primary products has been obsolescing recently, and fast. See Martin (2003) and Lindert and Williamson (2003: 249).

3. Although it only became apparent in the early 1990s, even sub-Saharan Africa is shifting out of mineral and agricultural exports and in to manufactures. In 1991 the share of manufactures in total exports was only 12 or 13 percent, while in 1998 it was almost 50 percent (Martin 2003: figure 6).

4. The World War I years are omitted.

5. This trend was calculated using a Hodrick-Prescott filter.

6. For important exceptions, see Mendoza (1997), Deaton and Miller (1996), Kose and Reizman (2001), Bleaney and Greenway (2001), and Hadass and Williamson (2003).

7. While greater volatility increases the need for international borrowing to help smooth domestic consumption, Catão and Kapur (2004) have shown recently that volatility constrained the ability to borrow between 1970 and 2001.

8. This sample covered about 90 percent of world population in 1900, and an even bigger share of world GDP and trade.

9. The poor periphery consists of 21 countries. Data exist for every country and every decade, except for one country-decade observation, yielding a sample of 125 (= $20 \times 6 + 5$). There are a few more missing observations from the interwar core, leaving 79 observations instead of the 84 (= 14×6) that would be available in a complete data set.

10. Note that we are holding fixed volatility in the terms of trade so we have, in effect, controlled for export concentration.

11. See the appendix tables in Blattman, Hwang, and Williamson (2004).

Chapter 7

This section draws heavily on Williamson (2005).

1. Figure 7.1 reports an unweighted average, but a trade-weighted or a GDP-weighted average yields the same trends. As I pointed out before, the thirty-five-country sample accounted for more than 90 percent of world GDP and trade in 1900.

2. The United States has always presented a problem to historians and economists alike. The canonical frontier economy with scarce labor and abundant resources, by 1900 it was also the world's industrial leader (Wright 1990) and a central market for the exports from the rest of the world, especially Latin America. So, while the United States was certainly a rich European offshoot, I allocate it to the industrial core.

3. In 1831, only 8.6 percent of the adult males in the United Kingdom had the right to vote, and even in 1866 the figure was still only 17.8 percent. These were, of course, the wealthy at the top of the distribution.

4. As late as 1940, the share of the adult male population voting in Latin America was never higher than 19.7 percent (Uruguay), while the lowest figures were for Ecuador, Bolivia, Brazil, and Chile (3.3, 4.1, 5.7, and 6.5 percent, respectively). Engerman, Haber, and Sokoloff (2000: table 2, p. 226).

5. To elaborate on a previous comment, industrial manufactures have been a rapidly rising share of Third World output and exports in the modern era. Among all developing countries, manufactures rose from about 15 percent of commodity exports in 1965 to about 82 percent by 1998 (Martin 2003: figure 3). Alternatively, the residual—agriculture and mining exports—fell from about 85 to 18 percent. Much of the Third World is now labor-abundant and natural resource–scarce so it exports labor-intensive manufactures. Thus, the growth of trade now helps it industrialize. No longer does the Third World just specialize in primary products.

6. Caution suggests using the phrase "was associated with" rather than "fostered." I press on without caution, but subject to this understanding.

7. The recent empirically based, openness-fosters-growth literature is huge. For two examples, see Sachs and Warner (1995) and Clemens and Williamson (2004b).

8. This argument can, of course, be extended to export duties in those cases where the periphery country controlled a significant share of world markets, and thus faced a (price-inelastic) downward sloping demand curve (e.g., Brazilian coffee).

9. Except, of course, that they could keep the price of imported raw material intermediates low by giving such imports tariff concessions, thereby raising the effective rate of protection on value added.

10. In a related paper on Latin America (Coatsworth and Williamson 2004a), capital inflows from Britain were added to the analysis for the years 1870–1913. This variable measured annual British capital exports to potential borrowing countries. Controlling for other factors, countries favored by British lending were shown to have had less need for tariff revenues and thus had lower tariffs. The variable does not appear here since our source (Clemens and Williamson 2004a) does not report the period 1914–1938. Although I do not report the results here, being on the gold standard was also associated with higher tariff rates, as predicted.

11. However, as time went on, periphery governments broadened their tax base to include taxes on urban transactions and property. To this extent, more urban countries would have had less need for tariff revenue, and thus could afford to be more "liberal." Thus, to the extent that the variable may also serve to confirm the importance of revenue motives, a negative offset to the hypothesized Stolper-Samuelson effects is possible. I acknowledge Domenica Tropeano for this idea.

12. When the "colony" dummy is replaced by a "tariff autonomy" dummy, thus to include Asian countries with those "unequal treaties" during the nineteenth century, the results are even stronger than those reported in table 7.1.

References

Acemoglu, D., S. Johnson, and J. A. Robinson (2001). "The Colonial Origins of Comparative Development: An Empirical Investigation." *American Economic Review* 91 (December): 1369–1401.

Acemoglu, D., S. Johnson, and J. A. Robinson (2002). "Reversal of Fortune: Geography and Institutions in the Making of the Modern World Income Distribution." *Quarterly Journal of Economics* 117 (4): 1231–1294.

Acemoglu, D., S. Johnson, and J. A. Robinson (2003). "The Rise of Europe: Atlantic Trade, Institutional Change, and Economic Growth." Unpublished paper, MIT (September 10).

Allen, R. C. (2001a). "The Great Divergence in Wages and Prices from the Middle Ages to the First World War." *Exploration in Economic History* 38 (October): 411–447.

Allen, R. C. (2001b). "Real Wages in Europe and Asia: A First Look at the Long-Term Patterns." Unpublished paper, Oxford University, United Kingdom. (August).

Bagchi, A. (1976a). "De-industrialization in India in the Nineteenth Century: Some Theoretical Implications." *Journal of Development Studies* 12 (October): 135–164.

Bagchi, A. (1976b). "Deindustrialization in Gangetic Bihar 1809–1901." In *Essays in Honour of Prof. S. C. Sarkar*. New Delhi: People's Publishing House.

Bagwell, K., and R. W. Staiger (2002). *The Economics of the World Trading System*. Cambridge, Mass.: MIT Press.

Bairoch, P. (1982). "International Industrialization Levels from 1750 to 1980." *Journal of European Economic History* 11 (Fall): 269–333.

Bairoch, P. (1989). "European Trade Policy, 1815–1914." In *The Cambridge Economic History of Europe, vol. III*, eds. P. Mathias and S. Pollard. Cambridge: Cambridge University Press.

Baland, J. M., and P. Francois (2000). "Rent-Seeking and Resource Booms." *Journal of Development Economics* 61 (2): 527–542.

Bassino, J.-P., and D. Ma (2004). "Japanese Wages and Living Standards in 1720–1913: An International Comparison." Paper presented to the conference Towards a Global History of Prices and Wages, Utrecht (August 19–21).

Berg, M. (1994). "Factories, Workshops and Industrial Organizations." In *The Economic History of Britain Since 1700: Volume 1: 1700–1860*, eds. R. Floud and D. McCloskey. Cambridge: Cambridge University Press.

Bértola, L. (2000). *Ensayos de Historia Económica: Uruguay y la región en la economia mundial 1870–1990*. Montevideo: Ediciones Trilce.

Bértola, L., and J. G. Williamson (2005). "Globalization in Latin America before 1940." In *Cambridge Economic History of Latin America*, eds. V. Bulmer-Thomas, J. Coatsworth, and R. Cortés-Conde. Cambridge: Cambridge University Press, forthcoming.

Blainey, G. (1966/1982). *The Tyranny of Distance: How Distance Shaped Australia's History*. Melbourne: Macmillan, revised 1982 ed.

Blattman, C., M. A. Clemens, and J. G. Williamson (2002). "Who Protected and Why? Tariffs the World Around 1870–1938." Paper presented to the *Conference on the Political Economy of Globalization*, Trinity College, Dublin (August 29–31).

Blattman, C., J. Hwang, and J. G. Williamson (2004). "The Impact of the Terms of Trade on Economic Development in the Periphery, 1870–1939: Volatility and Secular Change." NBER Working Paper 10600, National Bureau of Economic Research, Cambridge, Mass. (June).

Bleaney, M., and D. Greenway (1993). "Long-Run Trends in the Relative Price of Primary Commodities and in the Terms of Trade of Developing Countries." *Oxford Economic Papers* 45: 349–363.

Bleaney, M., and D. Greenway (2001). "The Impact of Terms of Trade and Real Exchange Rate Volatility on Investment and Growth in Sub-Saharan Africa." *Journal of Development Economics* 65: 491–500.

Bourguignon, F., and C. Morrisson (2002). "The Size Distribution of Income among World Citizens." *American Economic Review* 92: 727–744.

Brading, C. W. (1969). "Un analisis comparativo del costo de la vida en diversas capitales de hispanoamerica." *Boletin Historico de la Fundacion John Boulton* 20 (March): 229–263.

Brandt, L. (1985). "Chinese Agriculture and the International Economy 1870–1913: A Reassessment." *Explorations in Economic History* 22 (2): 168–180.

Brandt, L. (1993). "Interwar Japanese Agriculture: Revisionist Views on the Impact of the Colonial Rice Policy and Labor-Surplus Hypothesis." *Explorations in Economic History* 30 (3): 259–293.

Bulbeck, D., A. Reid, L. Tan, and Y. Wu (1998). *Southeast Asian Exports Since the 14th Century: Cloves, Pepper, Coffee, and Sugar.* Leiden, The Netherlands: KITLV Press.

Bulmer-Thomas, V. (1994). *The Economic History of Latin America Since Independence.* Cambridge: Cambridge University Press.

Caron, F. (1983). "France." In *Railways and the Economic Development of Western Europe, 1830–1914,* ed. P. K. O'Brien, 28–48. New York: St. Martin's Press.

Catão, L., and S. Kapur (2004). "Missing Link: Volatility and the Debt Intolerance Paradox." Unpublished paper, International Monetary Fund, Washington, D.C. (January).

Chaudhuri, K. N. (1978). *The Trading World of Asia and the English East India Company, 1660–1760.* Cambridge: Cambridge University Press.

Chaudhuri, K. N. (1983). "Foreign Trade and Balance of Payments 1757–1947." In *The Cambridge Economic History of India: Volume 2: c. 1757–c. 1970,* ed. D. Kumar. Cambridge: Cambridge University Press.

Clark, G. (2004). "The Condition of the Working-Class in England, 1200–2000: Magna Carta to Tony Blair." Unpublished paper, Department of Economics, University of California–Davis.

Clemens, M. A., and J. G. Williamson (2002). "Closed Jaguar, Open Dragon: Comparing Tariffs in Latin America and Asia before World War II." NBER Working Paper 9401, National Bureau of Economic Research, Cambridge, Mass. (December).

Clemens, M. A., and J. G. Williamson (2004a). "Wealth Bias in the First Global Capital Market Boom 1870–1913." *Economic Journal* 114 (April): 311–344.

Clemens, M. A., and J. G. Williamson (2004b). "Why Did the Tariff-Growth Correlation Reverse After 1950?" *Journal of Economic Growth* 9 (March): 5–46.

Clingingsmith, D., and J. G. Williamson (2004). "India's De-Industrialization under British Rule: New Ideas, New Evidence." NBER Working Paper 10586, National Bureau of Economic Research, Cambridge, Mass. (June 2004).

Coatsworth, J. H. (1979). "Indispensable Railroads in a Backward Economy: The Case of Mexico." *Journal of Economic History* 39 (4): 939–960.

Coatsworth, J. H. (1981). *Growth Against Development—The Economic Impact of Railroads in Porfirian Mexico*. Dekalb, Ill.: Northern Illinois University Press.

Coatsworth, J. H., and J. G. Williamson (2004a). "The Roots of Latin American Protectionism: Looking Before the Great Depression." In *FTAA and Beyond: Prospects for Integration in the Americas*, eds. A. Estevadeordal, D. Rodrik, A. Taylor, and A. Velasco. Cambridge, Mass.: Harvard University Press.

Coatsworth, J. H., and J. G. Williamson (2004b). "Always Protectionist? Latin American Tariffs from Independence to Great Depression." *Journal of Latin American Studies* 36 (May): 205–232.

Corbo, V. (1992). "Development Strategies and Policies in Latin America: A Historical Perspective." *International Center for Economic Growth, Occasional Paper* 22 (April): 16–48.

Corden, W. M. (1981). "The Exchange Rate, Monetary Policy and North Sea Oil: The Economic Theory of the Squeeze of Tradables." *Oxford Economic Papers* 33 (Supplement): 23–46.

Corden, W. M. (1984). "Booming Sector and Dutch Disease Economics: Survey and Consolidation." *Oxford Economic Papers* 36 (3): 359–380.

Corden, W. M., and F. H. Gruen (1970). "A Tariff That Worsens the Terms of Trade." In *Studies in International Economics*, eds. I. A. McDougall and R. H. Snape. Amsterdam: North Holland.

Corden, W. M., and J. P. Neary (1982). "Booming Sector and De-Industrialization in a Small Open Economy." *Economic Journal* 92 (December): 825–848.

Corpuz, O. D. (1997). *An Economic History of the Philippines*. Quezon City: University of the Philippines Press.

Crucini, M. J. (1994). "Sources of Variation in Real Tariff Rates: The United States 1900–1940." *American Economic Review* 84 (June): 732–743.

David, P. A. (1975). *Technical Choice, Innovation and Economic Growth*. Cambridge: Cambridge University Press.

Deaton, A., and R. I. Miller (1996). "International Commodity Prices, Macroeconomic Performance and Politics in Sub-Saharan Africa." *Journal of African Economics* 5: 99–191, Supplement.

DeLong, J. B., and A. Shleifer (1993). "Princes and Merchants: European City Growth before the Industrial Revolution." *Journal of Law and Economics* 39: 671–702.

Dercon, S. (2004). *Insurance Against Poverty* (Oxford: Oxford University Press).

De Vries, J. (1994). "The Industrial Revolution and the Industrious Revolution." *Journal of Economic History* 54 (June): 249–270.

Diaz-Alejandro, C. (1984). "Latin America in the 1930s." In *Latin America in the 1930s*, ed. R. Thorp, 17–49. New York: Macmillan.

Dixit, A. (1987). "Strategic Aspects of Trade Policy." In *Advances in Economic Theory: Fifth World Congress*, ed. T. F. Bewley. New York: Cambridge University Press.

Dobado, R., and G. A. Marrero (2005). "Corn Market Integration in Porfirian Mexico." *Journal of Economic History* 65 (1): 103–128.

Edelstein, M. (1982). *Overseas Investment in the Age of High Imperialism*. New York: Columbia University Press.

Engerman, S., S. Haber, and K. Sokoloff (2000). "Institutions, Factor Endowments, and Paths of Development in the New World." *Journal of Economic Perspectives* (Summer 2000): 217–232.

Estevadeordal, A., B. Frantz, and A. M. Taylor (2003). "The Rise and Fall of World Trade, 1870–1939." *Quarterly Journal of Economics* 118 (May): 359–407.

Fafchamps, M. (2004). *Rural Poverty, Risk and Development*. Chattenham: Edward Elgar.

Findlay, R. (1995). *Factor Proportions, Trade, and Growth*. Cambridge, Mass.: MIT Press.

Findlay, R., and K. H. O'Rourke (2003). "Commodity Market Integration, 1500–2000." In *Globalization in Historical Perspective*, eds. M. Bordo, A. M. Taylor, and J. G. Williamson, 13–62. Chicago: University of Chicago Press.

Flam, H., and M. J. Flanders (1991). *Heckscher-Ohlin Trade Theory*. Cambridge, Mass.: MIT Press.

Fogel, R. W. (1964). *Railroads and American Economic Growth: Essays in Econometric History*. Baltimore: Johns Hopkins Press.

Fogel, R. W. (1979). "Notes on the Social Saving Controversy." *Journal of Economic History* 39 (1): 1–54.

Frankenberg, E., K. Beegle, B. Sikoki, and D. Thomas (1999). "Health, Family Planning and Well-being in Indonesia during an Economic Crisis: Early results from the Indonesian Family Life Survey." RAND Labor and Population Program Working Paper Series 99-06, Rand Corporation, Santa Monica, CA.

Fremdling, R. (1983). "Germany." In *Railways and the Economic Development of Western Europe, 1830–1914*, ed. P. K. O'Brien, 121–147. New York: St. Martin's Press.

Gallup, J. L., A. Gaviria, and E. Lora (2003). *Is Geography Destiny? Lessons from Latin America*. Stanford, Calif.: Stanford University Press.

Gerschenkron, A. (1943). *Bread and Democracy in Germany*. Berkeley, Calif.: University of California Press.

Gerschenkron, A. (1962). *Economic Backwardness in Historical Perspective*. Cambridge, Mass.: Harvard University Press.

Goldsmith, R. W. (1985). *Comparative National Balance Sheets: A Study of Twenty Countries 1688–1978*. Chicago: University of Chicago Press.

Gómez Mendoza, A. (1982). *Ferrocarriles y Cambio Económico en España (1855–1913) un Enfoque de Nueva Historia Económica*. Madrid: Alianza.

Greasley, D., and L. Oxley (2004). "Refrigeration and Distribution: New Zealand Land Prices and Real Wages 1873–1939." Unpublished paper, University of Canterbury.

Green, A., and M. C. Urquhart (1976). "Factor and Commodity Flows in the International Economy of 1870–1914: A Multi-Country View." *Journal of Economic History* 36 (1): 217–252.

Grilli, E. R., and M. C. Yang (1988). "Primary Commodity Prices, Manufactured Goods Prices, and the Terms of Trade of Developing Countries: What the Long Run Shows." *World Bank Economic Review* 2: 1–48.

Habakkuk, H. J. (1962). *American and British Technology in the Nineteenth Century*. Cambridge: Cambridge University Press.

Habib, I. (1985). "Studying a Colonial Economy without Perceiving Colonialism." *Modern Asian Studies* 119 (3): 355–381.

Hadass, Y., and J. G. Williamson (2003). "Terms of Trade Shocks and Economic Performance 1870–1940: Prebisch and Singer Revisited." *Economic Development and Cultural Change* 51 (April): 629–656.

Harlaftis, G., and V. Kardasis (2000). "International Shipping in the Eastern Mediterranean and the Black Sea: Istanbul as a Maritime Center." In *Globalization Challenge and Economic Response in the Mediterranean Before 1950*, eds. Ş. Pamuk and J. G. Williamson. London: Routledge.

Harley, C. K. (1988). "Ocean Freight Rates and Productivity, 1740–1913: The Primacy of Mechanical Invention Reaffirmed." *Journal of Economic History* 48 (December): 851–876.

Hatton, T. J., and J. G. Williamson (1998). *The Age of Mass Migration: An Economic Analysis*. New York: Oxford University Press.

Hatton, T. J., and J. G. Williamson (2006). *Global Migration and the World Economy: Two Centuries of Policy and Performance*. Cambridge, Mass.: MIT Press, forthcoming.

Hawke, G. R. (1970). *Railways and Economic Growth in England and Wales, 1840–1870*. Oxford: Clarendon.

Hayami, Y. (1975). *A Century of Agricultural Growth in Japan*. Tokyo: University of Tokyo Press.

Hayami, Y., and V. Ruttan (1971). *Agricultural Development: An International Perspective*. Baltimore: Johns Hopkins Press.

Heckscher, E. F. (1919, 1991), "The Effect of Foreign Trade on the Distribution of Income." Translated and reprinted in *Heckscher-Ohlin Trade Theory*, eds. H. Flam and M. J. Flanders. Cambridge, Mass.: MIT.

Herranz-Loncán, A. (2003). "Railroad Impact in Backward Economies: Spain, 1850–1913." Unpublished paper, London School of Economics.

Huber, J. R. (1971). "Effect on Prices of Japan's Entry into World Commerce after 1858." *Journal of Political Economy* 79(3): 614–628.

Hurd, J. (1975). "Railways and the Expansion of Markets in India, 1861–1921." *Explorations in Economic History* 12 (3): 263–288.

Inikori, J. (2002). *Africans and the Industrial Revolution in England*. Cambridge: Cambridge University Press.

Irwin, D. A. (1998a). "Higher Tariffs, Lower Revenues? Analyzing the Fiscal Aspects of the Great Tariff Debate of 1888." *Journal of Economic History* 58 (March): 59–72.

Irwin, D. A. (1998b). "Changes in U.S. Tariffs: The Role of Import Prices and Commercial Policies?" *American Economic Review* 88 (September): 1015–1026.

Irwin, D. A. (1999). "Ohlin versus Stolper-Samuelson?" Paper presented to the Centennial Celebration of Bertil Ohlin, Stockholm, October 1999.

Issawi, C. (1966). *The Economy of the Middle East, 1800–1914*. Chicago: University of Chicago Press.

Jacoby, H. G., and E. Skoufias (1997). "Risk, Financial Markets, and Human Capital in a Developing Country." *Review of Economic Studies* 64 (July): 311–335.

Jensen, R. (2000). "Agricultural Volatility and Investments in Children." *American Economic Review* 90 (May): 399–404.

Jones, R. W. (1979). "A Three-Factor Model in Theory, Trade, and History." In *International Trade: Essays in Theory*, ed. R. W. Jones, 85–101. Amsterdam: North-Holland.

Kang, K. H., and M. S. Cha (1996). "Imperial Policy or World Price Shocks? Explaining Interwar Korean Living Standards." Paper presented to the Conference on East and Southeast Asian Economic Change in the Long Run, Honolulu, Hawaii (April).

Kimura, M. (1993). "Standards of Living in Colonial Korea: Did the Masses Become Worse Off or Better Off Under Japanese Rule?" *Journal of Economic History* 53 (3): 629–652.

Kindleberger, C. P. (1951). "Group Behavior and International Trade." *Journal of Political Economy* 59 (February): 30–46.

Korthals Altes, W. L. (1994). *Changing Economy in Indonesia: Volume 15: Prices (Non-Rice) 1814–1940*. The Hague, Netherlands: Royal Tropical Institute.

Kose, M. A., and R. Reizman (2001). "Trade Shocks and Macroeconomic Fluctuations in Africa." *Journal of Development Economics* 65 (1): 55–80.

Krueger, A. O. (1974). "The Political Economy of the Rent-Seeking Society." *American Economic Review* 64 (June): 291–323.

Krugman, P., and A. J. Venables (1995). "Globalization and the Inequality of Nations." *Quarterly Journal of Economics* 110 (November): 857–880.

Laffut, M. (1983). "Belgium." In *Railways and the Economic Development of Western Europe, 1830–1914*, ed. P. K. O'Brien, 203–226. New York: St. Martin's Press.

Landes, D. (1998). *The Wealth and Poverty of Nations*. New York: Norton.

Latham, A. J. H., and L. Neal (1983). "The International Market in Rice and Wheat 1868–1914." *Explorations in Economic History* 36 (2): 260–275.

Lewis, W. A. (1954). "Economic Development with Unlimited Supplies of Labour." *Manchester School of Economic and Social Studies* 22 (2): 139–191.

Lewis, W. A. (1970). *Tropical Development*. Evanston, Ill.: Northwestern University Press.

Lewis, W. A. (1978). *The Evolution of the International Economic Order*. Princeton, N.J.: Princeton University Press.

Lindert, P. H. (1994). "The Rise in Social Spending, 1880–1930." *Explorations in Economic History* 31 (January): 1–36.

Lindert, P. H. (2003). *Growing Public: Social Spending and Economic Growth since the Eighteenth Century*. Cambridge: Cambridge University Press.

Lindert, P. H., and J. G. Williamson (2003). "Does Globalization Make the World More Unequal?" In *Globalization in Historical Perspective*, eds. M. Bordo, A. M. Taylor, and J. G. Williamson, 227–271. Chicago: University of Chicago Press.

Ma, D. (2004). "Why Japan, not China, Was the First to Develop in East Asia: Lessons from Sericulture, 1850–1937." *Economic Development and Cultural Change* 52 (2): 369–394.

MacAlpin, M. B. (1979). "Dearth, Famine and Risk: The Changing Impact of Crop Failures in Western India, 1870–1920." *Journal of Economic History* 39 (1): 143–157.

Maddison, A. (1995). *Monitoring the World Economy 1820–1992*. Paris: OECD Development Centre Studies.

Maddison, A. (2002). *The World Economy: A Millennial Perspective*. Paris: OECD Development Centre Studies.

Magee, S. P., W. A. Brock, and L. Young (1989). *Black Hole Tariffs and Endogenous Policy Theory*. Cambridge: Cambridge University Press.

Márquez, G. (2002). "The Political Economy of Mexican Protectionism, 1868–1911." PhD thesis, Harvard University (March).

Martin, W. (2003). "Developing Countries' Changing Participation in World Trade." *World Bank Research Observer* 18 (20): 187–203.

Marx, K. (1977[1867]). *Capital, Volume 1*, translated by B. Fowkes. New York: Vintage Books.

Mayda, A. M., and D. Rodrik (2001). "Why Are Some People (and Countries) More Protectionist than Others?" NBER Working Paper 8461, National Bureau of Economic Research, Cambridge, Mass. (September).

Mendoza, E. (1997). "Terms of Trade Uncertainty and Economic Growth." *Journal of Development Economics* 54: 323–356.

Meissner, C. (2004). "A New World Order: Explaining the International Diffusion of the Gold Standard, 1870–1913." Unpublished paper, Cambridge University (April 15).

Mitchell, B. R. (1978). *European Historical Statistics 1750–1970*. New York: Columbia University Press.

Mitchell, B. R. (1993). *International Historical Statistics: The Americas 1750–1988*. 2nd ed. New York: Stockton Press.

Mitchell, B. R. (1998a). *International Historical Statistics: Europe 1750–1993*. 4th ed. London: Macmillan.

Mitchell, B. R. (1998b). *International Historical Statistics: Africa, Asia and Oceania 1750–1993*. 3rd ed. London: Macmillan.

Mitchell, B. R., and P. Deane (1962). *Abstract of British Historical Statistics*. Cambridge: Cambridge University Press.

Mohammed, S. S., and J. G. Williamson (2004). "Freight Rates and Productivity Gains in British Tramp Shipping 1869–1950." *Explorations in Economic History* 41 (April): 172–203.

Mokyr, J. (1993). *The British Industrial Revolution: An Economic Perspective*. Boulder, Colo.: Westview Press.

Murphy, K., A. Shleifer, and R. Vishny (1993). "Why Is Rent Seeking So Costly for Growth?" *American Economic Review* 83 (2): 409–414.

Murphy, K., R. Vishny, and A. Shleifer (1989). "Industrialization and the Big Push." *Journal of Political Economy* 97: 1003–1026.

Mussa, M. L. (1979). "The Two Sector Model in Terms of Its Dual: A Geometric Exposition." *Journal of International Economics* 9 (4): 513–526.

Myrdal, G. (1957). *Economic Theory and Underdeveloped Regions*. London: Duckworth.

Newland, C. (1998). "Economic Development and Population Change: Argentina 1810–1870." In *Latin America and the World Economy since 1800*, eds. J. Coatsworth and A. Taylor. Cambridge, Mass.: Harvard University Press.

North, D. C. (1958). "Ocean Freight Rates and Economic Development 1750–1913." *Journal of Economic History* 18 (December): 538–555.

Nurkse, R. (1953). *Problems of Capital Formation in Underdeveloped Countries*. New York: Oxford University Press.

Nurkse, R. (1959). *Patterns of Trade and Development: The Wicksell Lectures*. Stockholm: Almqvist and Wiksell.

Obstfeld, M., and A. M. Taylor (2003). "Globalization and Capital Markets." In *Globalization in Historical Perspective*, eds. M. Bordo, A. M. Taylor, and J. G. Williamson, 121–183. Chicago: University of Chicago Press.

Ocampo, J. A. (1994). "Una breve historia cafetera de Colombia, 1830–1938." In *Miniagricultura 80 años. Transformaciones en la Estructura Agraria*. Bogotá-Caracas-Quito: Tercer Mundo Editores.

O'Rourke, K. H. (1997). "The European Grain Invasion, 1870–1913." *Journal of Economic History* 57 (December): 775–801.

O'Rourke, K. H., and R. Sinnott (2001). "What Determines Attitudes Towards Protection? Some Cross-Country Evidence." In *Brookings Trade Forum 2001*, eds. S. M. Collins and D. Rodrik. Washington, D.C.: Brookings Institute Press.

O'Rourke, K. H., A. M. Taylor, and J. G. Williamson (1996). "Factor Price Convergence in the Late Nineteenth Century." *International Economic Review* 37(3): 499–530.

O'Rourke, K. H., and J. G. Williamson (1999). *Globalization and History*. Cambridge, Mass.: Cambridge University Press.

O'Rourke, K. H., and J. G. Williamson (2002a). "After Columbus: Explaining Europe's Overseas Trade Boom, 1500–1800." *Journal of Economic History* 62: 417–456.

O'Rourke, K. H., and J. G. Williamson (2002b). "When Did Globalization Begin?" *European Review of Economic History* 6 (April): 23–50.

O'Rourke, K. H., and J. G. Williamson (2005). "From Malthus to Ohlin: Trade, Growth and Distribution Since 1500." *Journal of Economic Growth* 10 (1): 5–34.

Overman, H. G., S. Redding, and A. J. Venables (2001). "The Economic Geography of Trade, Production, and Income: A Survey of Empirics." Unpublished paper, London School of Economics (August).

Pamuk, Ş. (1987). *The Ottoman Empire and European Capitalism, 1820–1913: Trade, Investment and Production*. Cambridge: Cambridge University Press.

Parthasarathi, P. (1998). "Rethinking Wages and Competitiveness in the Eighteenth Century: Britain and South India." *Past and Present* 158 (February): 79–109.

Prados, L. (2003). "Assessing the Economic Effects of Latin American Independence." Working Paper 03-12, Economic History and Institutions, Universidad Carlos III de Madrid, Madrid. (March).

Prados, L. (2004). "Colonial Independence and Economic Backwardness in Latin America." Working Paper 04-65, Department of Economic History and Institutions, Carlos III University (December).

Prebisch, R. (1950). *The Economic Development of Latin American and Its Principal Problems*. New York: United Nations Economic Commission for Latin America.

Pritchett, L. (1997). "Divergence, Big Time." *Journal of Economic Perspectives* 11 (3): 3–17.

Ramey, G., and V. A. Ramey (1995). "Cross-country Evidence on the Link Between Volatility and Growth." NBER Working Paper 4959, National Bureau of Economic Research, Cambridge, Mass.

Raychaudhuri, T. (1983). "The Mid-Eighteenth-Century Background." In *The Cambridge Economic History of India, II*, eds. D. Kumar and M. Desai. Cambridge: Cambridge University Press.

Reid, A. (1993). *Southeast Asia in the Age of Commerce 1450–1680: Volume Two: Expansion and Crisis*. New Haven, Conn.: Yale University Press.

Redding, S., and A. J. Venables (2000). "Economic Geography and International Inequality." *CEPR Discussion Paper 2568*.

Rodrik, D. (1995). "Political Economy of Trade Policy." In *Handbook of International Economics, Volume 3*, eds. G. M. Grossman and K. Rogoff, 1457–1494. Amsterdam: Elsevier.

Rogowski, R. (1989). *Commerce and Coalitions: How Trade Effects Domestic Political Arrangements*. Princeton, N.J.: Princeton University Press.

Rosenweig, M. R., and K. I. Wolpin (1993). "Credit Market Constraints, Consumption Smoothing, and the Accumulation of Durable Production

Assets in Low Income Countries: Investments in Bullocks in India." *Journal of Political Economy* 101 (2): 223–244.

Sachs, J., and A. Warner (1995). "Economic Reform and the Process of Global Integration." *Brookings Papers on Economic Activity* 1: 1–118.

Sachs, J., and A. Warner (2001). "The Curse of Natural Resources." *European Economic Review* 45 (May): 827–838.

Simmons, C. (1985). "De-Industrialization, Industrialization, and the Indian Economy, c. 1850–1947." *Modern Asian Studies* 19 (3): 593–622.

Singer, H. W. (1950). "The Distribution of Gains between Investing and Borrowing Countries." *American Economic Review* 40: 473–485.

Slaughter, M. J. (1995). "The Antebellum Transportation Revolution and Factor-Price Convergence." NBER Working Paper 5303, National Bureau of Economic Research, Cambridge, Mass. (October).

Steinberg, D. J. (1987). *In Search of Southeast Asia*. Honolulu: University of Hawaii Press.

Stemmer, J. E. O. (1989). "Freight Rates in the Trade between Europe and South America." *Journal of Latin American Studies* 21, pt. 1 (February): 22–59.

Stolper, W., and P. Samuelson (1941). "Protection and Real Wages." *Review of Economic Studies* 9: 58–73.

Summerhill, W. (2001). "Economic Consequences of Argentine Railroads, 1857–1913." Unpublished, UCLA.

Summerhill, W. (2005). "Big Social Savings in a Small Laggard Economy: Railroad-Led Growth in Brazil." *Journal of Economic History* 65 (1): 72–102.

Thomas, D., K. Beegle, E. Frankenberg, B. Sikoki, J. Strauss, and G. Teruel (2004). "Education in a Crisis." *Journal of Development Economics* 74 (June): 53–85.

Tomlinson, B. R. (1993). *The New Cambridge History of India: III, 3: The Economy of Modern India 1860–1970*. Cambridge: Cambridge University Press.

Tornell, A., and P. R. Lane (1999). "The Voracity Effect." *American Economic Review* 89 (1): 22–46.

Tornell, A., and A. Velasco (1992). "The Tragedy of the Commons and Economic Growth: Why Does Capital Flow from Poor to Rich Countries?" *Journal of Political Economy* 100: 1208–1231.

Vamplew, W. (1971). Railways and the Transformation of the Scottish Economy." *Economic History Review* 24 (1): 37–54.

Whitcombe, E. (1983). "Irrigation." In *The Cambridge Economic History of India: Volume 2: c. 1757–c. 1970*, ed. D. Dumar. Cambridge: Cambridge University Press.

Williamson, J. G. (1997). "Globalization and Inequality, Past and Present." *World Bank Research Observer* 12 (2): 117–135.

Williamson, J. G. (1998). "Globalization, Labor Markets and Policy Backlash in the Past." *Journal of Economic Perspectives* 12 (Fall): 51–72.

Williamson, J. G. (1999). "Real Wages, Inequality, and Globalization in Latin America Before 1940." *Revista de Historia Economica* 17 (special number): 101–142.

Williamson, J. G. (2000). "Globalization, Factor Prices and Living Standards in Asia Before 1940." In *Asia Pacific Dynamism 1500–2000*, ed. A. J. H. Latham. London: Routledge.

Williamson, J. G. (2002a). "Two Centuries of Globalization: Backlash and Bribes for the Losers." *WIDER Annual Lecture*, Copenhagen (September 5).

Williamson, J. G. (2002b). "Land, Labor and Globalization in the Third World 1870–1940." *Journal of Economic History* 62 (1): 55–85.

Williamson, J. G. (2005). "Explaining World Tariffs 1870–1938: Stolper-Samuelson, Strategic Tariffs and State Revenues." In *Eli Heckscher, 1879–1952: A Celebratory Symposium*, eds. R. Findlay, R. Henriksson, H. Lindgren, and M. Lundahl. Cambridge, Mass.: MIT Press.

Williamson, J. G., and P. H. Lindert (1980). *American Inequality: A Macroeconomic History*. New York: Academic Press.

Wright, G. (1990). "The Origins of American Industrial Success, 1879–1940." *American Economic Review* 80 (September): 651–668.

Yamazawa, I. (1975). "Yushutsunyu Kakakuhisu" (The indices of export and import prices). In *Kindai Nihon no Keizai Hatten*, eds. K. Ohkawa and R. Minami. Tokyo: Tokyo Keizai Shinposha.

Yasuba, Y. (1978). "Freight Rates and Productivity in Ocean Transportation for Japan, 1875–1943." *Explorations in Economic History* 15: 11–39.

Yasuba, Y. (1996). "Did Japan Ever Suffer from a Shortage of Natural Resources Before World War II?" *Journal of Economic History* 56 (3): 543–560.

Abbreviations

AHG	Austria-Hungary	JPN	Japan
ARG	Argentina	KOR	Korea
AUS	Australia	MEX	Mexico
BRA	Brazil	NOR	Norway
BUR	Burma	NZD	New Zealand
CAN	Canada	PER	Peru
CEY	Ceylon	PHL	Philippines
CHL	Chile	POR	Portugal
CHN	China	RUS	Russia
COL	Colombia	SPA	Spain
CUB	Cuba	SRB	Serbia
DEN	Denmark	SWE	Sweden
EGY	Egypt	TAI	Taiwan
FRA	France	THA	Thailand
GER	Germany	TKY	Turkey
GRC	Greece	UK	United Kingdom
IDN	Indonesia	URU	Uruguay
IND	India	USA	United States
ITA	Italy		

Index